# Tribalism in Crisis

# TRIBALISM IN CRISIS

## Federal Indian Policy, 1953–1961

**Larry W. Burt**

University of New Mexico Press
*Albuquerque*

**Library of Congress Cataloging in Publication Data**

Burt, Larry W., 1950–
  Tribalism in crisis.

  Bibliography: p.
  Includes index.
  1. Indians of North America—Government relations—
1934–    . 2. United States—Politics and government—
1953–1961. I. Title.
E93.B975 1982      323.1′197′073      82–11069
  ISBN 0–8263–0633–0

Manufactured in the United States of America.
International Standard Book Number 0-8263-0633-0.
Library of Congress Catalog Card Number 82–11069.
*First edition*

*To Grace*

# Contents

# Preface

Throughout United States history, the land base and sovereignty of Native American groups declined as whites expanded across the continent. Americans removed Indians militarily until the end of the nineteenth century and thereafter turned to a policy of assimilating them into the dominant culture and system.

This policy was temporarily halted in the 1930s when John Collier, commissioner of Indian affairs under President Franklin Roosevelt, attempted to reverse the loss of land and allow Indians to adjust to modern industrial society at their own pace and within their own cultures. But forces emerged during World Warr II that led to further United States expansion and to another assault on remaining tribal sovereignty and holdings. A bloc of conservative western congressmen known as terminationists began advocating a return to a policy of assimilation and withdrawal of federal supervision and services to Native Americans.

This study describes and analyzes attempts to implement their ideas after Republican victories in the 1952 elections gave them significant political strength. Terminationists actually achieved only limited success in the long run. By the mid-1950s extreme conservatism was abating and opposition growing, as the impact of the new policy became clear. Many Native Americans charged that it destroyed their culture and communities. Local and state governments began to realize that federal withdrawal would heap unwanted social and economic burdens on them. And in some cases conservationists fought against dismantling reservations for fear that the removal of lands from federal regulation and their subsequent development would damage the ecology. Near the end of the period considerable opposition also came from a resurgence of Indian nationalism and racial consciousness, owing in part to the recent rise of a black civil rights movement.

The Democratic administration of John F. Kennedy, which took office in 1961, generally rejected the Republican policies. But significant sentiment in favor of termination still existed in Congress and severe reservation problems remained—with no clear solution in sight.

Many people assisted in the preparation of this study, and their contributions merit special recognition. I would like to thank the staff at the University of Toledo Library, especially director Leslie Sheridan, who helped arrange the purchase of the Glenn Emmons papers on microfilm from the University of New Mexico General Library. Thanks also go to personnel at other libraries and archives, including the Toledo–Lucas County Public Library, the University of Michigan Graduate Library in Ann Arbor, the Northern Montana College Library, the National Archives, and the Dwight D. Eisenhower Library in Abilene, Kansas.

In addition, I would like to extend appreciation to Suzanne Julin, who provided invaluable assistance in working with the taped interviews in the South Dakota Oral History Center in Vermillion, to Northern Montana College, which supported my visit to that research institution, and to other people who either helped me make contacts for my own oral history projects or consented to be interviewed personally or through the mail, including Joe Callahan, Michael O'Donnell, Walter McDonald, Joe McDonald, Madison Coombs, the late Glenn Emmons, and Orme Lewis. Perhaps the greatest debts are owed to Dr. W. Eugene Hollon, whose careful reading of this manuscript vastly improved its quality and whose friendship and example of first-rate scholarship will always be appreciated, and to my wife, K. Grace, who helped type preliminary drafts and supported me in more ways than I could ever enumerate.

# Introduction

From the beginning of North American colonization, Europeans pushed Indians out of the path of their expansion. But as long as Native Americans retained the ability to stop their advance or to exact bloody retribution, the two sides negotiated treaties governing the geographic divisions between them. By the 1870s the power relationship had grown increasingly one-sided and Congress substituted less legally binding agreements for treaties, no longer recognizing tribes as having the same stature as foreign countries. Then, over the next several decades Native Americans were militarily driven onto reservations, which constantly shrank as reports of wealth attracted hordes of fortune-seeking outsiders and led to violent confrontations and demands for still further cessions.[1]

Reform movements emerged out of a reaction against such depredations and promoted a scheme to divide communally held reservations into 160-acre allotments and teach Indians to farm. They believed that the only way to protect Native Americans from annihilation was to absorb them into the dominant society. Several other groups supported the idea because the land that remained after the division of reservations could be sold. Frontiersmen, farmers, and a wide variety of entrepreneurs naturally wanted to buy the property and exploit its resources. At the same time, the army hoped that the receipts from sales could be used to defray the costs of supporting western Indians.[2]

The pressure for severalty finally resulted in the passage of the General Allotment Act, also known as the Dawes Act, in 1887. This represented another significant step away from bilateral relationships between tribes and the United States by dealing with Indians as individuals rather than as members of autonomous groups. Under its provisions, title to individual plots would re-

1

main in trust with the United States government for twenty-five years to protect the Indian from losing his land in deals with more experienced whites before he learned how to manage personal property within the dominant culture. At the end of the period, a Native American would receive a fee-simple title, although the president could extend the trust period if he deemed it necessary. The Indian would then be granted United States citizenship, which many reformers felt would provide valuable instruction in the art of civilization.[3]

As it turned out, presidents routinely postponed the expiration of trust arrangements. Nonetheless, the Indian land base dwindled through tax defaults and sales to non-Indians as the Bureau of Indian Affairs (BIA) granted fee-patent titles either by request or, in some cases after 1917, without prior consent. Moreover, few Native Americans became farmers, since much of their land was not arable and most lacked the tools, resources, and necessary knowledge. The traditional cultures of some groups, such as the Sioux in the northern plains, considered farming women's work and thus discouraged an agricultural way of life.[4]

As conditions continued to deteriorate, various Indian interest groups and some Native Americans agitated for the expansion of political rights and freedom from BIA control in the hope that Indians could better improve themselves through their own initiative. Some Indians had received citizenship through military service or allotment under the Dawes Act, but when Native American participation in World War I called for a gesture of appreciation, the granting of American citizenship to all Indians seemed to patriotic Americans an appropriate response to both goals. Congress thus enacted legislation in 1924 that made Native Americans citizens. However, this action further complicated the sovereignty issue between tribes and the United States. Some considered it another step in the assimilation into American life, while many Indians rejected citizenship and refused to shed their identity or culture.[5]

Two years later Secretary of the Interior Hubert Work asked the Brookings Institution to survey the situation on reservations in response to recent critical reports. Some of the specialists who worked on the project adhered to an ideology of cultural pluralism, or relativism. Many social scientists, especially in the new field of anthropology, had replaced the previously accepted view of man's universal advancement in stages from savagery to civilization with an existential rejection of any single route by which mankind had developed. They concluded that cultures were not to be judged. Rather, they existed to serve peoples' social and psychological needs in a variety of environments. And since Indian cultures were so deeply instilled and unable to undergo drastic change without severe strain, the inevitable adjustment of Indians to a modern industrial society should be on their own terms and within the context of their own cultures. This philosophy served as the foundation of the Meriam Report in 1928, which blamed much of the dismal poverty and hopelessness among Indians on the loss of their land and on the forced cultural change stemming from the allotment policy.[6]

When John Collier became Indian commissioner in 1933, he attempted to end the policy of assimilating individual Native Americans and, instead, tried to incorporate the ideology of cultural pluralism into the administration of Indian affairs. He prodded Congress into enacting the Wheeler-Howard bill, known as the Indian Reorganization Act (IRA), the next year. The IRA put a stop to further allotment, extended trusts indefinitely, authorized the return of "surplus" lands undisposed of under the Dawes Act, and funded the acquisition of additional holdings. To improve and protect the economic base of tribes, the legislation instituted conservation measures such as strict cutting restrictions in forests and the regulation of livestock grazing on grasslands. The measure also established a Revolving Fund credit program to promote the economic development of reservations by tribes. In a significant recognition of tribal self-government, Indians were given the right to organize, draw up constitutions, elect officials, and retain considerable independent authority.[7]

For many reasons, Collier only partly realized his goals. Some Indians were already assimilated at this point and considered the IRA a retrogressive measure. Extreme traditionalists resented the intrusion of white concepts of democratic elections into their governmental structures, usually because elections usurped the authority and position of hereditary tribal chiefs. Non-Indian westerners who leased native land resisted any attempts to encourage Indians to use their own resources. Moreover, Congress frequently blocked Collier's program by refusing to appropriate adequate funding.[8]

By the mid-1940s opposition to Collier's ideas and policies had gained considerable strength. The World War II experience had generated a spirit of unity and consensus in the country, which made the presence of a distinct Indian culture and sovereignty unacceptable to many. In addition, as the United States and Russia drifted deeper into Cold War hostility, an almost paranoiac sense of insecurity developed out of the belief that Soviet communism represented a threat to the nation's safety. This insecurity resulted in an intolerance toward anything that deviated from mainstream values. In such an atmosphere many found traditional Indian communal social structures offensive since they seemed too similar to the dreaded socialist systems that the United States was supposedly resisting. Even some Native Americans who had become relatively acculturated while serving in the armed forces got caught up in the era's super-patriotism and began denouncing Collier's policies.[9]

A strong conservative reaction against the rapid changes brought about by the New Deal under President Franklin Roosevelt also contributed to the change in attitude toward Indian society. Many congressmen resolved to end the trend toward enlarged federal budgets and mushrooming bureaucracies. They considered the BIA one of many bloated agencies and therefore sought to get the bureau out of the "Indian business" and to set Native Americans free from misguided intellectuals and government regulations and supervision. Moreover, recent technological innovation and material advancement reinforced the conservative faith in free enterprise and the belief that progress came only through industrialization led by private entrepreneurs. Many assumed from an ethnocentric point of view that everyone wanted to be modernized, and they maintained that Collier's policies encouraged primitive peoples to remain as aborigines and "museum pieces" instead of being "civilized" as they should be.[10]

Perhaps most important, federal expenditures in the West vastly increased during the war and resulted in a tremendous economic boom throughout the region. Farming, stockraising, lumber, mining, manufacturing, and service industries sought out every resource and parcel of land to take advantage of the high prices from the boom and extract a profit. This naturally put pressure on the remaining Indian holdings. Not only did economic interests want the property, but rapid development also spurred growth by state and local governments and a subsequent search for new sources of revenue to pay for their proliferating expenditures. Influential westerners thus called for the removal of trust restrictions on Indian land so it could be taxed and Native Americans would pay their "fair share" toward the support of an area.[11]

Out of this situation emerged a bloc of conservative congressmen known as terminationists who advocated an end to trust arrangements and any remaining tribal sovereignty, the integration of Native Americans into the dominant culture, and federal withdrawal from all Indian affairs. They introduced bills at the request of constituents that would remove title restrictions on particular plots of land so local interests could acquire them. They fought against Collier's programs and forced him in 1943 to begin plans for federal withdrawal on each reservation. Two years later the beleaguered commissioner resigned in despair.[12]

In 1946, Congress enacted the Legislative Reorganization Act. One effect of this act was to ensure that future Indian policies would reflect the needs of the recent boom in the western economy. The House Committee on Indian Affairs was merged with committees on public lands, territories, irrigation and reclamation, mines, and insular affairs to form a new Committee on Interior and Insular Affairs. The bill likewise combined the Senate Committee on Indian Affairs and committees on public lands and surveys, mines, territories, and insular affairs into a Committee on Interior and Insular Affairs. These changes made the welfare of Indians an even more remote consideration in the formation of policy affecting them, since committees under the powerful influence of various western economic interests replaced those that had been exclusively concerned with Native Americans.[13]

Congress passed another bill that same year designed to help pave the way for federal withdrawal from Indian affairs. The Claims Commission Act created a special court that allowed tribes to present a legal case against the United States for inadequate compensation in land cessions, without first having to request special enabling legislation, as previously required. Although Congress acted partly in response to considerations of justice and a desire to save time and money, it also intended the move as a final settlement between old antagonists so that federal responsibility could be ended.[14]

Throughout the late 1940s congressional terminationists escalated their attacks on the BIA, while bureau officials struggled to retain the main features of the IRA. In early 1947 the Senate Committee on the Post Office and Civil Service conducted hearings on federal employees in a search for ways to reduce the number of workers on the government payroll. It called on the BIA to show progress in the withdrawal planning recently demanded by Congress. Assistant Indian Commissioner William Zimmerman gave the committee a list of tribes divided into three categories according to the degree of their acculturation, economic condition, and willingness to cooperate. Those in the first group were allegedly ready for quick release from supervision and services, those in the second would need ten years, and those in the third would require an indefinite period of preparation.[15]

Zimmerman envisioned a type of federal withdrawal similar to that initiated by Collier at congressional insistence near the end of his term. Tribes would function legally as corporations, retain the autonomy and self-governing authority spelled out in the IRA, and be rehabilitated on their reservations and within the framework of their own cultures. However, congressional terminationists seized on Zimmerman's testimony, and for the next decade they would cite it as justification for the timeliness of their own brand of withdrawal requiring less government expenditure and allowing greater development of native resources by non-Indian outsiders.[16]

A disaster in the Southwest that same year lent new momentum to the Collier-Zimmerman version of how to deal with Native Americans and their reservations. Major winter blizzards hit the Navajos and Hopis, requiring a massive government airlift to prevent widespread starvation and death among already poverty-stricken people. The publicity given to the Indians' plight, set off against a background of Marshall Plan dollars being sent to foreign countries, resulted in a temporary marketability in Congress for large-scale federal rehabilitation efforts on individual reservations. In 1950, Congress passed the Navajo-Hopi Act, also known as the Long Range Act, which authorized $88,570,000 over a ten-year period for various health and education programs, plus construction projects, roads, and resource development.[17]

The Department of the Interior launched an investigation into conditions among the Navajos and concluded that the indigence on the reservation was due to the fact that the land could only support 35,000 of the 55,000 inhabitants. Although based upon outdated BIA resource surveys, this "surplus population" theory helped absolve the government of responsibility for the recent catastrophe and also served as the rationalization for many of the policies promoted by conservative terminationists. If reservations could maintain only a fraction of their population, then it was futile to spend money on local rehabilitation. The "surplus" of Indians therefore should be transferred to industrial cities where they could find employment. Accordingly, Congress approved a relocation program to aid Navajos in the move to urban areas. This program was also viewed as a way of assimilating Indians and raising their social and economic status after other attempted programs had failed, especially education.[18]

Terminationists scored a major victory in 1950 when President Harry Truman selected the former head of the War Relocation Authority, a post-war agency that dismantled Japanese internment camps, as commissioner of Indian affairs. Dillon Myer purged the BIA of most pro-Collier people, reorganized the agency to make it more responsive to withdrawal efforts, and did as much as he could to achieve the goals of terminationists administratively. Furthermore, in 1952 he launched Operation Relocation, expanding the program begun initially as part of the Navajo-Hopi Act to other tribes as well.[19]

After the precedent set by the Navajo-Hopi Act, many other tribes naturally requested similar aid, and in response Myer created a division of program within the BIA to help plan for rehabilitation on various reservations. But since Congress was unwilling to finance any more such programs, the new branch focused its activity on the few groups which had enough money to pay for their own projects or tried to incorporate terminationist goals by planning for legislation that would simply withdraw all government responsibility for particular groups and end their special status and any remaining sovereignty.[20]

# The Selection of an Indian Commissioner

While Dillon Myer was commissioner many Native Americans grew fearful of the emphasis on federal withdrawal from Indian affairs. Dissatisfaction focused not only on Myer but also on the Democratic party and the Truman administration. As the 1952 presidential election approached, some Indians worked for a change in political leadership. Dan Madrano of the National Congress of American Indians (NCAI), the largest Native American organization, urged the Republicans at their nominating convention to promise the Indians an opportunity to select the next commissioner. The Republicans attempted to capitalize on the unrest, and in their platform they vaguely stated that the administration would "consult and confer" in the appointment.[1]

Not all of those unhappy with Indian policy looked to Republicans for support. Oliver La Farge, president of the Association on American Indian Affairs (AAIA), the largest interest group of non-Indians, supported the Democratic nominee Adlai Stevenson. La Farge initially backed Eisenhower, but switched late in the race when Stevenson declared that all laws, policies, and choice of officials should be based on Indian consent.[2]

Competition between parties was especially heated in New Mexico, where Native Americans had only recently won the right to vote. In the years since the Indian Citizenship Act of 1924 all states except Arizona and New Mexico had extended the franchise to their native residents. Decisions in separate court cases in 1948 forced the southwestern states to conform, and politicians adjusted their strategies accordingly. Indeed, New Mexican Republicans now looked to the Indian vote to swing the state away from the traditionally strong Democrats.[3]

The influential Gallup banker and politician Glenn L. Emmons quickly grasped the importance of the approximately 47,000 new votes in his state. He had initially tried to convince Eisenhower forces at the 1952 Republican national convention to send the nominee to the thirty-first Inter-Tribal Indian Ceremonial, an annual all–Native American event held in Gallup, New Mexico. But the General's campaign was too disorganized at the time for a definite commitment.[4]

Shortly after returning to New Mexico, Emmons solicited the help of the state's Republican governor, Edwin L. Mechem. Republican campaign leaders were scheduled to meet soon in Denver, so the two New Mexicans traveled there, where Mechem arranged a dinner with the Republican governor of Colorado, Dan Thornton. The Eisenhower strategists had just arrived in Denver and were conveniently dining at a table next to Emmons and the two governors. Thornton took advantage of the opportunity and set up a meeting.[5]

Campaign leader and Nebraska senator Fred Seaton presided over the subsequent conference. He was at first reluctant to pursue the idea, mentioning that because Mechem had been a supporter of Ohio senator Robert Taft at the convention, Eisenhower owed him nothing. The New Mexico governor then turned the meeting over to Emmons, who had served as an Eisenhower delegate, and the banker tried to convince the political strategists of his scheme. Seaton first offered to send vice-presidential nominee Richard Nixon into New Mexico, but Emmons held out until the Eisenhower staff agreed to send its presidential candidate to Gallup for the early August celebration.[6]

Emmons worked very hard in preparation for the future president's arrival. He arranged for a greeting line at the airport to include governors of the various Pueblo reservations in the area as well as a group of Navajo war veterans. Navajo Tribal Chairman Sam Ahkeah was to meet the general upon landing and introduce him to others in the greeting line.[7]

To everyone's surprise, the airplane arrived about an hour earlier than the appointed time of 12:00 noon on August 10. Television cameras and local Indians were not yet in place, so Emmons insisted that the pilot delay the arrival; he flew over the Grand Canyon until everything was in order. After the initial greetings and a colorful procession into town, Eisenhower expressed vague dissatisfaction with present Bureau of Indian Affairs (BIA) policy in a public address before the crowds of Indians and also reminded the audience of their new civic responsibility to vote.[8]

The effort proved very successful. Navajos constituted about 60 percent of the Indian population and voted overwhelmingly for Eisenhower. One local newspaper placed the figure at 95 percent. By a margin of roughly 30,000 the GOP gained a state it had not won in a presidential contest since 1928.[9]

Eisenhower's victory stimulated a flurry of activity, as interested groups and individuals struggled to influence the selection of the commissioner. Administrations commonly divided many political appointments among state party organizations, and New Mexico Republicans naturally wanted the post for their state. They realized the competitive advantage in agreeing on a single choice, and most of them quickly united behind the state's public welfare director and Mechem's representative on the Governors' Interstate Indian Council (GIIC), Alva Adams Simpson. The three New Mexican members of the Republican National Committee and the state party's county chairmen followed Mechem's lead in endorsing Simpson.[10]

Individual Indians and various organizations also came out on behalf of Simpson. Although they hardly constituted a unified voice, they based their support on the hope for a change in BIA policy toward the kind of tribe-by-tribe rehabilitation programs typified by the Navajo-Hopi Act of 1950. NCAI director Madrano backed Simpson partly because he knew that New Mexico Republicans would have considerable influence over the selection, and he wanted to be part of a winning team. He also saw in Simpson's political record the possibility for federal efforts toward rehabilitation on the nation's reservations. As a GIIC member, Simpson had lobbied Congress for higher appropriations for the BIA. He especially tried to convince legislators to grant more money to the perennially underfunded Navajo-Hopi program. Simpson's lack of success, however, caused some Navajos to charge that he was willing to settle for second-rate schools and facilities on their reservation.[11]

Meanwhile, a group of businessmen began campaigning for Glenn Emmons. New Mexican friends and associates of Emmons, led by publisher and radio station owner Frank Rand, initiated the effort. Since Eisenhower had surrounded himself with many industrialists and financiers, they readily found avenues into the inner circles of the new administration team. Soon after the election, Rand recommended Emmons to Sidney J. Weinberg, a New York investment banker whose close relationship with top Eisenhower officials made him an important "contact" in appointment matters. In mid-December Emmons expressed an interest in the commissionership in a telegram to the President-elect, noting the support of prominent businessmen. About the same time Rand solicited the help of a close colleague of Weinberg's, Owen-Illinois Glass Company board chairman William E. Levis. The president of Rand's radio station, the head of Gallup's chamber of commerce, and other area business leaders petitioned Levis to promote Emmons. Levis channeled all such endorsements to Weinberg, who then passed them to the Eisenhower headquarters. The businessmen's campaign soon gained an even more significant figure when the president of the United States Chamber of Commerce, Laurence F. Lee, came out in active support.[12]

The Navajo Tribal Council quickly joined the movement for Emmons. The council consisted primarily of the most assimilated and most successful Navajos, many of whom were sheepherders who bought goods from the same local businessmen leading the commissionership campaign. These traders frequently co-signed loans from Emmons's bank, since reservation Indians could not use property in trust status as collateral. Thus, close ties existed between those Navajos able to take advantage of the white economic world and the area's commercial and financial establishment. Many local Indians saw Emmons as their spokesman.[13]

On December 31, the council bought a full-page ad in the *Santa Fe New Mexican* declaring that it wanted "a businessman as commissioner and no more social workers, anthropologists, or reformers." This statement reflected the council's traditional lack of sympathy with the Indian Reorganization Act (IRA) and the liberal reforms of the 1930s.[14] An opposition faction composed of poorer and less-assimilated Navajos living west of Cuba, New Mexico immediately sent a petition with 1200 signatures to the president-elect. They accused the council of acting as a tool of the BIA and aligned Emmons with local commercial interests whom they felt had taken advantage of them.[15]

By early 1953 the contest had intensified and ten additional candidates had emerged. A group of Oklahoma Indians launched a vigorous crusade to have a Native American selected, most of them supporting Choctaw tribal chief Harry T. W. Belvin. Other Oklahoma tribal members flooded Eisenhower's office with petitions on Belvin's behalf. Nevertheless, Simpson appeared to be the front runner when NCAI director Madrano claimed that eighty-nine tribes representing 200,000 Indians had passed resolutions supporting him. Emmons's only tribal endorsement remained that of the Navajo council.[16]

After the inauguration, Eisenhower still had not made a choice. Rumors circulated among Indians that Myer would be retained, but the March 19 announcement of the unpopular commissioner's resignation laid that controversy to rest. Throughout the early spring, administration officials found themselves trying to ease the fear of a continuation of Myer's policies. Appearing on the National Broadcasting Company's "Meet the Press" on April 5, the new secretary of the interior, Douglas McKay of Oregon, said that he was not in sympathy with current policies. He declared that the government should prepare Native Americans for full citizenship rights, but he did not detail how he intended to achieve that goal.[17]

Clues coming out of the administration in May revealed some of the criteria used in the selection process as well as the nature of upcoming policy. A United Press International story quoted officials close to McKay as saying that the secretary would avoid appointing a Native American because the constituents of such a commisioner would expect him to do more for Indians than Congress would fund. This statement naturally dampened expectations, but activities to influence the choice continued nonetheless.[18]

Most of the responsibility for the final decision went to the new assistant secretary of the interior for public lands management, Phoenix lawyer Orme Lewis, whose administrative domain included the BIA. To abide by the Republic campaign pledge to consult Native Americans on the selection, Eisenhower sent Lewis on a cross-country trip to visit representatives of over 150 tribal groups, undoubtedly for appearances, since the assistant secretary later referred to the trip as "relatively unimportant because of time constraints." Although he never announced the results of his survey, he later informed the White House staff that nearly 60 tribes had endorsed Simpson and only 2 had endorsed Emmons. Officials privately led supporters of the New Mexican public welfare director to believe that he would get the post. Secretary McKay gave the impression at a meeting with Madrano at a Dickerson College seminar in Pennsylvania that Simpson

would become the next commissioner. The administration, however, preferred someone with a business background. This was
not an isolated example of the way administration personnel were
selected; writers frequently referred to Eisenhower's corporate-
dominated cabinet as "nine millionaires and a plumber." Accompanied by Stanley Pratt of the Republican National Committee,
Lewis met with Glenn Emmons in Washington in mid-June and
left satisfied with the banker's politics and positions on Indian
affairs.[19]

Indeed, the President's choice for commissioner fit in well with
the rest of the administration. Emmons had a long history in
business, finance, and politics. Born in Atmore, Alabama in 1895,
he moved with his family ten years later to Albuquerque, New
Mexico, where his father owned a furniture store. While still in
school Glenn worked as an elevator operator and later as a loco-
motive fireman for a lumber company. In 1919 after discharge
from the Air Force he went to Gallup, New Mexico and gained
employment as a bookkeeper at Gallup State Bank.[20]

Emmons's career and his leadership in the business community
and politics advanced quickly. In 1921 he organized a chamber
of commerce in Gallup and served as its unpaid secretary until
the following year when it became a permanent organization with
a full-time staff. At about the same time Glenn and his older
brother John began working for the First National Bank of Gallup, with John serving as vice-president and Glenn as cashier.
Glenn became politically active in the Democratic Party, setting
himself in opposition to his former employer, the powerful Republican owner of Gallup State Bank, Gregory Page. In 1926 he
ran unsuccessfully for county treasurer and then switched to the
Republican Party two years later because of a growing friendship
and political alignment with New Mexico's Senator Bronson Cutting. That same year Glenn advanced to vice-president of First
National Bank, and John became president.[21]

In 1935, when John retired from his position, Glenn moved into
the top post. Thereafter, the younger Emmons expanded his activities even further. In 1944 he ran for governor of New Mexico
on an anti–New Deal, pro-business platform but was defeated in
the Republican primary. Over the next decade he served as the
president of the Gallup Kiwanis Club, commander of the Gallup
American Legion post, president of the New Mexico Bankers As-

sociation, a member of the University of New Mexico's Board of Regents, and treasurer of the American Bankers Association.[22]

Perhaps most important, Emmons shared with fellow businessmen in the Eisenhower administration a vision of progress defined as industrial development led by private entrepreneurs. Like most other twentieth-century conservatives, he saw government as an obstacle to achieving the general good and looked to organizations like chambers of commerce, Rotary, Kiwanis, and Optimists for political, social, and economic leadership.[23]

State political patronage also contributed significantly to the decision. Although most of New Mexico's Republican officials had endorsed Simpson, Eisenhower owed them little because most had supported Senator Robert Taft for the presidential nomination.[24] Furthermore, Emmons had helped capture a traditionally Democratic state, as well as having served as an alternate Eisenhower delegate to the national convention.

Perhaps more important, the administration needed the political cooperation of the New Mexican congressional delegation, especially Clinton Anderson. The powerful senator enjoyed considerable influence in the White House. As a conservative Democrat, he frequently cooperated with Republicans. Throughout the campaign to appoint an Indian commissioner, Anderson denied persistent rumors that he was maneuvering against Simpson in favor of Emmons. In the controversial election for the state's other senate seat in 1952, Democrat Dennis Chavez had opposed General Patrick J. Hurley. The Senate later investigated allegations of voting fraud, but a verdict was not expected until May or June 1953. One political observer maintained that the Eisenhower administration was delaying the decision on a commissioner until the outcome of the investigation. Hurley supported Simpson, and although Chavez did not publically declare for anyone, he had been a friend and neighbor of Emmons's since childhood. The Senate eventually gave the seat to Chavez, but not until a year later.[25]

Meanwhile, the growing restlessness of Indians forced the administration to act with only an "informed guess" on the results. On July 9, Lewis told the White House of his choice for Indian commissioner, and Secretary McKay formally recommended Emmons to Eisenhower. Administration officials and New Mexico Republicans then turned their attention to healing the wounds opened by the recent controversy. In an effort to avoid the appearance of personal defeat, Governor Mechem requested that McKay announce Simpson's withdrawal from contention. Also, Assistant Secretary Lewis attempted to time the procedures to win confirmation of Emmons as quickly as possible. Republican Hugh Butler of Nebraska, chairman of the Senate Committee on Interior and Insular Affairs, therefore agreed to schedule the confirmation hearings one day after the announcement of Emmons's selection and without the customary week's notice.[26]

When the president submitted the nomination to the Senate on July 15, newspapers reported that Simpson had withdrawn because of a recent salary increase and critical duties in his present position.[27] Later that same day Senator Butler opened the confirmation proceedings with the explanation of the need to accommodate Emmons's busy schedule. Thus, several witnesses who otherwise might have opposed the nomination were unable to attend, and the few committee members present had little interest in Indian affairs. With no substantial opposition to Emmons present, the questioning generally proved very shallow. When Henry Jackson of Washington asked Lewis about his consultation efforts and the preferences of various Indian associations, the assistant secretary could not remember their choices.[28]

The next day Eisenhower's office announced the decision publicly. The committee reported favorably on the nomination, and the clerk scheduled a floor vote that afternoon. According to procedural rules, the Senate could act on the same day that a name came out of committee only when there was unanimous consent. But a brief delay followed when Republican William Langer of North Dakota objected, charging that too many Indian commissioners had come from New Mexico and none from the Dakotas.[29]

The delay gave the opposition to Emmons time to reorganize its forces. The *Arizona Republic* asserted in an editorial that nothing in the banker's background qualified him for the job. It questioned how he could serve the interests of the various tribes when his only experience with Native Americans consisted of contact with one political faction of Navajos and membership in the Inter-Tribal Indian Ceremonial Association, a group it compared to a chamber of commerce. In addition, Indians from Oklahoma flooded Congress and local newspapers with letters charging that the president had violated his campaign promise.[30]

The newly elected director of the NCAI, Frank George, channeled damaging information and letters from disgruntled Indians to Senator Langer and to the perennial iconoclast from Oregon, Independent Wayne Morse. George maintained that western special interests backed Emmons and wanted Indian-held lands. He pointed especially to key supporter Laurence Lee, claiming that Lee held investments in a large livestock company and sought to remove government regulation from areas of possible economic expansion.[31]

Langer quickly became the rallying point for others who opposed confirmation. Some critics charged Emmons with having embezzled from his Gallup bank during the 1930s. On July 20, Langer announced that he would vigorously fight the nomination and that he had at least two witnesses who would soon reveal shocking information on the matter. Three days later the senator from North Dakota attacked the procedures surrounding the confirmation hearings. He called on the committee to reopen the questioning and determine if Emmons "embezzled $60,000 or helped to create a shortage in his bank, or didn't." Senator Anderson jumped to the defense and inserted into the *Congressional Record* many letters from supporters testifying to the banker's good character. Emmons also came out fighting and called the charges "the most astounding lies I have ever heard." He accused Langer of leaving himself an excuse to hide behind when proven wrong by appending the phrase "or didn't" at the end of his well-publicized attack.[32]

Despite such a spirited defense, the allegations necessitated new hearings to avoid charges that the administration had short-circuited the confirmation process. The committee scheduled them for July 28, which left little time for the opposition to put together a case or bring witnesses to Washington. But the issue was moot, as senate opposition faded. Langer quickly renounced his adamant position, declaring that he sought only to guarantee proper procedure and would probably vote for Emmons.[33]

It became clear at the second hearing that only the allegation of embezzlement aroused senatorial concern. The charges originated when Emmons's brother and banking partner, John, borrowed $40,000 from powerful New Mexico Senator Bronson Cutting. Critics contended that the two used the money to hide shortages from the federal examiner sent to determine an insti-

tution's soundness following the bank holiday in 1933. Although
the investigator uncovered some irregularities, the United States
attorney considered them insufficient to bring charges. Emmons
testified that he and his brother had deposited the money in his
brother's bank in Durango, Colorado to bolster its cash position.[34]

With few records available after over twenty years and no one
for the opposition pursuing the allegations, the committee found
little reason to doubt Emmons's business colleagues when they
vouched for his honesty and integrity. But Native Americans who
appeared against the banker bitterly denounced the practice of
deceit by the Eisenhower administration. They attempted to ex-
pose Emmons as a man who intended to follow a policy of federal withdrawal in spite of Republican pledges to the contrary.
But broken campaign promises mattered little to senators, and
they confirmed Emmons the next day.[35]

The controversy subsided for a time, but the aftermath of the
stormy debate lingered. Because of attacks leveled at his support
of Emmons, Chamber of Commerce head Laurence Lee decided
not to attend the new commissioner's swearing-in ceremony nor
to visit him later in his office. In an effort to avoid further criticism of his association, he thereafter met with Emmons in hotel
rooms. Not until a year later did Lee dare to assist openly in
Indian affairs, as Emmons had hoped he could. The National Congress of American Indians (NCAI) also made an important concession by removing Frank George as director. With the source
of much of the controversy eliminated, the NCAI now looked
forward to better relations with the new BIA leadership.[36]

# Formation of a Policy

As contestants vied for the commissionership, policymakers hurried to reverse New Deal programs and to implement their own ideas on the integration of Indians into American life. The 1952 elections gave GOP conservatives control of both branches of government, and general consensus prevailed for the first time since Collier's reign. Moreover, westerners dominated the committees on interior and insular affairs. The assignments were not highly prized, and since both committees dealt primarily with western resources, the seats had gone to congressmen from districts with a special interest in the committees' work.[1]

Most of these western, conservative Republicans were ardent nationalists. Definitions of nationalism admittedly differ, and reflections of the phenomenon change according to time and circumstance. But in general, nationalism can be considered "a state of mind in which the supreme loyalty of the individual is felt to be due the nation state" or, more precisely, "the commitment to the preservation and advancement of the social entity known as the nation [which] takes priority over the commitment to all other values and beliefs, [and] where other values and beliefs are judged in terms of their relevance to this end."[2] American expressions of nationalism were of course not new, even in their use as justification for displacing Native Americans or for diminishing their sovereignty, since such attitudes ran throughout the history of the westward frontier process. But nationalism surged within the United States after World War II in large part as a consequence of Cold War competition with Russia, and western conservatives expressed an extreme version of it. This led to less tolerance of institutions and cultural forms that were seen as outside of the American mainstream. Conservatives believed that the Indian Citizenship Act of 1924 had placed Native Americans

19

under the same governing authority as other U.S. citizens and rendered independent sovereignty, bilateral relations, and treaty provisions all irrelevant.[3]

Thus the only solution to the "Indian problem" was assimilation into the dominant society. One of the key policymakers in the early Eisenhower years, Assistant Interior Secretary Orme Lewis, summarized the governing attitude of the period when he later wrote,

Basically, they [Indians] are Americans and ought to become a part of us for their own good and for the benefit they can give us. . . . I do not think that they are as well off as they would have been if they had been absorbed into the population. I have utterly no patience with those who think more about Indian culture than they do about Indians. The world is made up of people who overran others, as a result of which we have great nations. America is an outstanding example of that, and the Indians are just as capable of becoming a part of the whole thing and lending their blood to ours as any of the others. The culture will live as it deserves to.[4]

Notions of limited federal government and libertarian economic individualism existed along with nationalism in conservative thought. Republicans of the 1950s saw land restrictions and BIA services as violations of a social and economic system based upon property rights and private enterprise. Progress for Native Americans would come only when society freed them from restrictions and allowed them to compete with other Americans in the common marketplace.[5]

In the area of land tenure, for example, conservatives refused to recognize the legitimacy of separate tribal landholding status or trust arrangements. They saw little difference between native holdings and public-domain lands and favored opening all such federally controlled areas to private ownership in order to expand opportunities for business enterprise. They naturally expected some loss of acreage as Indian land was converted into fee-simple title but believed that the retention of holdings by Indians should depend on productivity with the marketplace as the ultimate determinant.[6]

Special treatment allegedly gave Indians the impression that they could always remain "wards." Conservatives gave the term "ward" a welfare connotation in describing native dependence on material aid and services from the federal government. It actually originated in the early 1830s when Supreme Court Justice John Marshall used the word to define the sovereignty relationship between tribes and the United States. He concluded that Indian groups retained some sovereignty, but it was limited by the greater sovereignty of the United States, a situation resembling a ward/guardian relationship.[7]

The administration's fiscal conservatism would soon affect nearly all BIA programs. Upon taking office the new secretary of the interior immediately trimmed over $12 million from the bureau's projected budget for fiscal 1954. New construction projects took the biggest cuts, since he assumed that such services would end before reaching completion.[8]

Secretary McKay also ordered the BIA to make all programs more self-supporting and businesslike. Accordingly, operation and maintenance charges assessed Indian users on certain irrigation projects would increase and thus reduce government subsidization. The interest rates on loans through the BIA would rise from 2 percent to 4 or 5 percent to ensure the recovery of the program's operating costs.[9]

Few loans were available, however, because under the new policies the credit division would hold loans to a minimum, owing to past delinquency in repayment. Outside of problems with loans to Alaska fish canneries because of bad salmon runs, the delinquency rate actually compared reasonably well with that experienced by private lenders. Nevertheless, the Department of the Interior insisted that Congress never intended the credit program as a subsidy and therefore tightened its availability to all groups. The amount of money lent under the Revolving Fund dropped by about 60 percent in 1953 and even more dramatically in the next two years. The BIA repossessed all tangible assets in delinquency cases to further reduce losses, but most of the goods eventually were almost given away since no market existed for them.[10]

Emmons and the BIA encouraged the use of private lending institutions to fill the vacuum as the bureau withdrew its credit services. But most Indians experienced great difficulty in obtaining loans from outside sources. They could rarely post the necessary security because the trust lands that were usually their only sizable assets could not be used as collateral. Emmons lifted this prohibition for a time but had to reverse himself when insurance companies raised questions which led to the determination that no law sanctioned the foreclosure of trust lands. Moreover, local prejudices usually prevented Indians from establishing the reputations needed for credit based only on character.[11]

To solve these problems Emmons promoted a scheme whereby tribes would deposit funds in a bank, which in return for a carrying charge would use the money to back loans to Native Americans. Naturally, these arrangements would work only when a group had the money in the first place. Also, the plan imposed economic decision making by non-Indian bankers since they would either grant or deny loans. The Indian Reorganization Act's (IRA) Revolving Fund program had given tribal bodies control over their own activities. Under this approach the Blackfoot Tribe in Montana deposited $50,000 in the Conrad Products Credit Association as a loan guarantee. BIA superintendent James Stewart convinced Indians on the Colorado River reservation to make a similar agreement with a local bank.[12]

At the same time the congressional Indian affairs subcommittees quickly agreed upon a general legislative strategy for dismantling the bureaucracy which they believed encouraged dependence, retarded progress, and delayed Indian citizenship. They concluded that Congress should accelerate the removal of trust status on land and repeal laws that applied only to Indians. It should terminate all supervision and services to some tribes in certain states and to all tribes in others. Finally, it should transfer many BIA functions to states or to other federal agencies. Commissioner John Collier had also used the transfer tactic in the 1930s and 40s but with a different goal in mind. He turned to it as a way of enabling Indians to acquire quickly access to services essential for personal and group progress, especially after Congress proved reluctant to fund adequately his development programs. The emphasis of Congress again in the 1950s perhaps revealed a higher priority given to eliminating the BIA rather than the services it rendered. This priority may give some credence to accusations by opponents of federal withdrawal that the major motive was the eradication of the agency that sometimes blocked easy access to Indian resources.[13]

Significant congressional action came in early summer when Representative William Henry Harrison of Wyoming introduced House Concurrent Resolution 108, which laid the foundation for a major policy reversal. It declared goals of ending wardship status, phasing out the BIA, and making Native Americans subject to the same rights and responsibilities as other citizens. The Department of the Interior would receive a mandate to submit legislation by January 1, 1954, for the termination of the Flathead, Klamath, Menominee, Potawatomi, and Turtle Mountain Chippewa tribes as well as all groups within California, Florida, New York, and Texas. Although few House members were even aware of the measure, it passed without debate August 1 on the consent calendar amid a long list of minor bills. The Senate endorsed it three days later after little or no discussion.[14]

Two other measures did not fare as well. One of these promoted by the House subcommittee called for the transfer of all health activities affecting Indians to the Public Health Service (PHS) in the Department of Health, Education, and Welfare. Various medical organizations had recently called for such a move in hopes that PHS could do more to alleviate deplorable situations on reservations. The idea also fit neatly into plans for dismantling the BIA, but disagreement within the administration prevented it from getting out of the full committee. The Department of the Interior objected to fragmenting a system of closely related social services among different agencies and preferred a plan that would integrate Native Americans into the health systems of non-Indian communities.[15]

The second proposed legislation was sponsored by Representative Wesley D'Ewart of Montana and was designed to deal with the problem of Indian unwillingness to apply for removal of land-title restrictions. It called for the automatic fee patenting of allotments as Native Americans reached twenty-one years of age. The measure encountered stiff opposition from those who would be affected, and its failure was assured when the Department of the Interior's solicitor ruled that such action was unconstitutional without consent of the owners.[16]

The successful passage in mid-August of two noncontroversial bills, however, lent support to the "liberation" argument in the promotion of federal withdrawal. Both repealed obsolete and discriminatory legislation dating from the previous century. Public Law 277 lifted the federal liquor prohibition on reservations and granted tribes a local option on sales of alcohol. Public Law 281 dropped bans on the sale of munitions, farming tools, and clothing in "hostile country" (the term used in the nineteenth century law) and eliminated restrictions on individual Indian livestock transactions.[17]

A measure with many more ramifications concerned the transfer to the states of law-and-order jurisdiction on reservations. After Chief Justice Marshall's precedent-setting decisions in the 1830s in favor of tribal retention of at least some independent sovereignty, most Indian "domestic dependent nations" maintained their own courts and police agencies. For almost a full century tribes shared responsibility with the federal and state governments in a bewildering tangle of jurisdictional authority. National law applied in ten of the most serious kinds of crimes, while the states exercised control in civil disputes between Indians and whites and in offenses committed by natives off the reservation. Tribal courts held jurisdiction in most other matters.[18]

Problems naturally resulted, but fractionated law-and-order responsibility was not necessarily the primary cause. The effectiveness of Indian institutions varied considerably. Some tribes retained a much stronger sense of self-government than others and therefore worked harder to maintain functioning courts and police departments. Those in better financial condition generally had a much better law enforcement system. The less affluent groups not only experienced high crime rates partly because of poverty, but they also had to rely on the BIA's grossly underfunded and ineffective law enforcement services.[19]

Regardless of the cause, lawlessness near reservations posed a threat to white neighbors, which combined with the general assault on tribal sovereignty, greatly contributed to the argument in favor of state jurisdiction over Indian areas. Congress had already passed several bills in the late 1940s giving certain states authority over specific groups within their borders, and by the early 1950s there was considerable congressional support for nationwide state takeover of all reservations. The Department of the Interior insisted, however, on a tribal consent clause and a state-by-state approach to deal better with individual situations.[20]

In the 1953 congressional session separate bills were introduced involving Indians in California, Minnesota, Nebraska, Oregon, and Wisconsin. The House subcommittee combined these proposals into one measure and promoted it as part of its larger program of federal withdrawal from Indian affairs. By this time the department had dropped its demand for tribal consent in favor of prior consultation with groups involved. While the subcommittee extended state jurisdiction over reservations in the five states, it exempted the Red Lake Chippewas of Minnesota, the Warm Springs Band of Oregon, and the Menominees of Wisconsin, who had objected to the change. In the most controversial move, Representative Hugh Butler of Nebraska added sections which allowed any other state to assume jurisdiction merely by legislative statute or by constitutional changes if necessary. The federal government had required some western states upon entrance into the United States to include disclaimers in their constitutions that renounced any claim to jurisdiction over reservations within their boundaries. Public Law 280 passed on August 15 after virtually no debate in the two houses.[21]

But an outcry quickly followed as opponents charged that Public Law 280 wiped out much of the remaining tribal sovereignty and rights guaranteed in numerous treaties. They accused Congress of rushing it through at the end of the session so that few would notice. Indians expecially feared discrimination at the hands of state officials and also the loss of hunting and fishing rights if forced to conform to sports and recreation regulation. John Collier's Institute of Ethnic Affairs and the National Congress of American Indians (NCAI) voiced strong opposition to the lack of provisions for referendum by Native Americans. The American Civil Liberties Union called for a veto, and even Eisenhower expressed disapproval of the arbitrary nature of the bill. He characterized it as unchristian and suggested an amendment that would provide for tribal consent. Nevertheless, he signed it and thus contributed to a prolonged debate over the direction of Indian affairs.[22]

The retention of nearly all top-level BIA personnel from the Myer years, together with recent congressional action, convinced many Indians that the administration's new policies were no better than those of President Truman. In the aftermath of the struggle between policies based on "consent" and "consultation," the administration sent Emmons to various western reservations to counter the growing anxiety and opposition among Native Americans. At each stop the new commissioner drew on the authority and prestige of the "Great White Father" by reading from a letter sent by the president. The message reiterated campaign pledges to consider Indian "thoughts, needs, and aspirations" in the creation of programs affecting them. Emmons avoided statements of policy, tried to ease apprehension, and stressed that his role was to listen and consult. He assured those concerned about the withdrawal of services that they would be continued for years. And he emphasized to the "long hairs" worried about the destruction of Indian identity that no one would be forced to give up his culture.[23]

While the commissioner was allaying the Indians' fears, the BIA was hurriedly preparing termination bills for the next legislative session as mandated in House Concurrent Resolution 108. Thus the bureau was caught between the congressional drive to establish quickly a policy-making precedent and promises of consultation. Emmons therefore called in the area directors and superintendents of the groups to help draw up rough drafts of legislation, or "discussion bills." He then sent copies to the field with instructions to officials to talk over the proposals with the various tribes and local and state governments "so that no Indian or anybody else could properly say that the BIA was trying to thrust a particular bill down their throats." After some revisions the drafts reached Congress in time for the January start of the 1954 session.[24]

Meanwhile, the Department of the Interior began a study of the BIA to devise procedures for administrative implementation of withdrawal plans as well as policies to fit the bureau budget into the national program of economic austerity. In early October Assistant Secretary Orme Lewis appointed Walter Bimson, chairman of the board of Phoenix's Valley National Bank and a "political gymnast of extraordinary ability" according to Lewis, to head the investigation. Other members included Robert D. Lutton of the Santa Fe Railroad, U. R. Johns of Sears, Roebuck and Company, and three BIA officials. Bimson's visits to many reservations provided an illusion of Indian participation, and Secretary McKay announced upon completion of the committee's work in January of 1954 that its recommendations would result in greater services.[25]

But the overriding objectives of the Bimson commission clearly were to cut the budget and to phase out the BIA. Many suggestions merely called for a continuation or expansion of procedures already in practice. These included putting services on a self-sustaining basis or transferring various functions to states, tribal governments, or other federal agencies. The committee further advised consolidations of several area offices and branches within the bureau, as well as reductions in the number of staff technicians. It urged greater use of the relocation program, since it cost as much to maintain services on reservations as it did to move Indians into cities. Regarding the building of educational facilities under the 1950 Navajo-Hopi Act, the report suggested postponing construction of high-cost boarding schools. Instead, there should be a concentration on semipermanent structures that could accommodate as many students, but at a per-capita reduction of from $6000 to $800. Realizing its recommendations would be unpopular, the study called for the development of a public relations campaign to gain support. The Bimson Report would not only make possible a more effective coordination of tactics with Congress, it would also provide a blueprint for bureau programs and priorities for the next several years.[26]

# 4

# The Drive to Terminate
# Various Tribes

As the 1954 session opened, congressional proponents of federal withdrawal prepared for speedy passage of the first group of termination bills called for in House Concurrent Resolution 108. Lack of interest in the matter enabled a handful of members to direct the effort. The 83d Congress gave the chairmanship of the Senate Indian Affairs Subcommittee to Republican Arthur V. Watkins of Utah. Watkins quickly took charge and scheduled a series of hearings on the proposals to begin in mid-February. In an unusual move to ensure prompt action, he arranged joint sessions of both House and Senate subcommittee members.[1]

The deeply religious and nationalistic Mormon senator held a singular view of progress. He saw the continuing plight of Indians as a result of their failure to follow the path toward development forged by the nation's dominant culture. Watkins denied that any obstacles prevented their successful absorption into the American way of life. Discrimination against Native Americans did not exist in his view. In fact, on several occasions during the hearings Watkins angrily challenged Indian witnesses to offer him an example of discrimination. Although a decade later a new Commission on Civil Rights would document numerous such cases, at the time most of the Native Americans sat silent and avoided a confrontation with the man who exercised extraordinary power over their fates. Moreover, recent congressional surveys detailing the middle-class items owned by Indians seemed to prove their preparedness. Watkins considered past treaties irrelevant and therefore refused to recognize dual citizenship. Congressional authority, he believed, was sufficient to end trust arrangements. Assimilation naturally embraced duties as well as privileges, including the responsibility to "pay for civilization" through taxation. Watkins also believed that Indian opponents fought the status change only to avoid taxes and to retain free services and that Indian membership and rights groups resisted out of the fear of being disbanded once their clients were assimilated.[2]

Most of the BIA-drafted bills considered at the hearings differed only in detail to conform to individual situations. Each tribal member would receive an interest in group assets, a reversal of the traditional legal priority in which common property status took precedence over personal rights. Tribal rolls would close on the date of enactment to establish a fixed list of those eligible for a share. Every bill also stipulated that Indians had the right to draw up the roll, but the secretary of the interior would retain ultimate authority in disputed cases. Most bills also extended options to tribes concerning the future status of their land and economic organization. They could sell everything and dispense the proceeds, organize into a corporation under state law, or choose a private trustee to replace the BIA. If they failed to act, the secretary would appoint a trustee to dispose of all holdings and distribute the returns.[3]

Trust status on individual allotments was to end on a specific date, although the transitional period varied. In the meantime the secretary could sell or partition heirship lands at the request of any one owner.[4] Each bill likewise would include provisions for the continued protection by private trustee of property belonging to minors and incompetents. Upon the arrival of the final termination date, all tribal members would become subject to the same laws as non-Indians, and Indian Reorganization Act (IRA) charters, along with all separate sovereignty and governing authority, would be revoked.[5]

Watkins began the hearings with six small bands of Paiutes and Shoshones in his home state on the Shivwitts, Kanosh, Koosharem, Indian Peaks, Skull Valley, and Washakie reservations. Most of the Indians lived in little towns away from their reservations and subsisted on seasonal migrant farm work or public assistance. Although House Concurrent Resolution 108 had made no mention of them, the BIA prepared a bill for their termination at the request of the Utah congressional delegation. Many did not speak English or have much formal education. The bureau provided few services, so the change would mainly involve land titles. When their BIA superintendent inquired in the summer of 1953 if they favored termination, tribal leaders responded negatively. Later Senator Watkins visited the area and tried to change their minds. Early the next year, a representative from Triumph Uranium and Oil Company, Charles Harrington, met with members of four of the groups for the same purpose.[6]

Mineral companies could exploit native resources at substantially less cost without intervention by the BIA. With bureau regulations and sales restrictions eliminated, they could buy the land or negotiate leases without going through the usual procedure of advertising and awarding extraction rights to the highest bidder, which Harrington had previously tried unsuccessfully to do. Even though the bureau allowed some of the most lucrative leasing arrangements in the business, corporations anticipated arranging still better deals from indigent and undereducated Indians than from experienced government bureaucrats.[7]

Before favorably reporting the proposal to the full Congress, the subcommittee dropped the Skull Valley and Washakie bands from the bill. The two groups had vehemently opposed termination, and the subcommittees noted that "they may not understand the legislation." After the revelations concerning the role of the oil company representative, which critics had quickly noted in the press, the congressmen also extended Indian subsurface titles for ten additional years. Subcommittee members claimed the support of the remaining four groups for the measure "as far as [they could] ascertain," based on a letter from Harrington to Watkins and on correspondence to the Association on American Indian Affairs (AAIA) from the business manager of the Kanosh group, for which Harrington served as counselor, according to the Indians' BIA superintendent.[8]

The joint subcommittees turned next to the approximately 450 poor and very traditional Alabama-Coushatta Indians of Texas. The BIA virtually ignored them except for subsidizing the education of their children in local public schools and extending the right to use Indian hospitals and schools in Oklahoma.[9] The state of Texas paid for a few other services, but the bureau had never administered any harvesting of their timber nor encouraged any form of economic enterprise. As early as 1951 local officials began discussions with the Alabama-Coushattas regarding the possibility of the State Forest Service taking over management of the reservation to bring in an income from sustained-yield cuts.[10] The Tribal Council favored the plan, but the BIA interpreted its position as a request for termination.[11]

When the Indians learned that they were the subjects of proposed legislation that would remove the trust status of their lands, they immediately sent a delegation to meet with their local congressman. Representative John Dowdy shortly thereafter introduced a separate substitute bill which would allow the Texas tribe to continue attending BIA schools and hospitals. He hoped it would help win those concessions on a bill he felt he could not defeat. During the subsequent hearings, Dowdy bitterly criticized the bureau for making it appear that the tribe wanted termination, and for its disgraceful treatment of people too poor to send delegates to Washington in their own defense and unprepared to be cast out on their own. The bill reported out by the subcommittees included the retention of the right to use BIA schools and hospitals for another five years and bowed to Indian requests that they have final approval over any future disposition of their lands. Also it differed substantially from the bureau's standard format by simply transferring trust arrangements to the state of Texas.[12]

When representatives of the small groups under the Potawatomi area field office in Kansas appeared at the hearings, members of the subcommittees witnessed the strongest protests to date. Chairwoman of the Prairie Band of Potawatomi Minnie Evans led an angry defense of her tribe's treaty guarantees against what she saw as the inevitable loss of lands. Kickapoo leader Vestana Cadue not only objected to a change in status and to the removal of the few services already performed by the BIA, but also demanded more aid to alleviate her people's deplorable poverty. An off-reservation faction of the Iowa band favored liquidation of tribal property, but the rest of the group overwhelmingly disapproved of their termination under the bureau-drafted proposal being considered. The only other tribes included in the measure, the Sac and Fox, did not take a position, but it made no difference since the subcommittee killed the bill after such bitter resistance.[13]

Although House Concurrent Resolution 108 had not included the approximately 2100 Indians in sixty small bands in western Oregon, Emmons instructed the bureau to draw up a termination bill covering all of them after it had obtained resolutions favoring the idea from several tribal councils. Some of the Indians were attracted by the temporary relief from poverty that would result after liquidating tribal property, and most felt that termination was inevitable anyway since local non-Indians wanted their land.

Others were convinced by the BIA's contention that termination would eliminate discriminatory laws such as prohibitions against drinking in Oregon bars, purchasing firearms, or marrying whites. However, the vast majority of the affected Indians neither participated in the decision nor was even aware of termination action until afterwards. Of those who did know what was happening, only a few fully understood that it implied an end to all special services, the elimination of their legal status, and the abrogation of their hunting and fishing rights.[14]

The BIA and congressional terminationists vigorously promoted the proposal covering the western Oregon bands when it came before the subcommittees at the joint hearings. They contended that the transition would be simple because the Indians were well integrated into the area's economy, life-style, and community structure and because they received few bureau services anyway. Most western Oregon Native Americans were indeed more assimilated than others since they had previously lost the largest part of their land base and had to work as common laborers in neighboring communities. The Indians, however, did not think of themselves as being as integrated as terminationists believed. They displayed few outward signs of traditional life-style but knew that deep economic, educational, and cultural differences still separated them from the rest of the people in the area.[15]

The level of Indian assimilation, together with the disunity among the many scattered groups, discouraged collective opposition and made it easier for subcommittee members to support their termination. About 800 of the Native Americans living near the town of Empire maintained no ties with tribal governments, while the 700 loosely affiliated as the Confederated Tribes of Siletz and the remaining 500 organized under the title Grand Ronde Community lacked a common heritage. They existed primarily as creations of Indian Reorganization Act (IRA) charters. Thus, the subcommittees changed the proposal covering western Oregon groups very little and reported out a bill that closely conformed to the standard BIA format.[16]

Residents of the Klamath Reservation in Oregon also lacked a high degree of unity and tradition. The tribal organization consisted of about 2000 Klamaths, Yahooskins, Snakes, and Pitt River Indians. They lived a comparatively assimilated life-style on and around the nearly one-million-acre reserve which contained some of the most valuable ponderosa pine in the region. Although wealthy by Indian standards, they relied heavily on services provided or contracted by the BIA. The Tribal Council funded over two-thirds of the benefits, but outsiders dominated higher level supervisory and managerial functions. The Indians' relative affluence and integration into the local community made them appear to be perfect candidates for federal withdrawal.[17]

Local economic and business interests also contributed to the rising tide in favor of termination. The bureau had traditionally allowed outside companies to cut heavily in the Klamath forest, bringing large profits to lumbermen but not to the Indians. Recently the amount of timber available had been significantly reduced, and companies were forced to operate at production levels far below capacity since they had already overcut on their holdings. They demanded the opening of more federally controlled land to private ownership to remove it from restrictive sustained-yield management and bring it under Oregon law, which required that only a few small trees remain after a harvest to ensure eventual regrowth. Similarly, area cattlemen objected to the close control of grazing privileges that since the 1930s had increasingly prevented them from using Indian grasslands without payment. Many local civic and business groups also looked forward to the new money that would come into county coffers after the removal of nontaxable status from Indian property.[18]

Thus, when a very vocal minority faction of primarily off-reservation Klamaths, led by Mr. and Mrs. Wade Crawford, began agitating for liquidation, termination proponents placed them high on the list in policy planning. In 1948, Portland BIA area director E. Morgan Pryse ordered superintendent Raymond Bitney to prepare for withdrawal of property trusteeship. But support from the National Congress of American Indians (NCAI) enabled the tribe successfully to oppose the effort. Former Indian commissioner Dillon Myer failed in a later attempt to push a termination bill through Congress, but pressure on the Klamaths increased after the passage of House Concurrent Resolution 108 in 1953. The case "monopolized the time at the Bureau," according to Assistant Interior Secretary Orme Lewis in referring to the first few years of the Eisenhower administration. This monopolization was undoubtedly due at least in part to the Interior Department's view that Klamath termination was central to the implementation of its overall Indian policy, but Lewis also attributed it to "tribal political difficulties and the sad physical state of the Indians there, occasioned by inactivity on their part."[19]

Most of the Indians did not fully understand termination or take part in the decision making. However, the Tribal Council consistently rejected any bill drawn up by the BIA and tried to substitute provisions that would include greater native control over the withdrawal process and leave their organization and authority intact. If a measure had to pass, the council preferred one that merely allowed the malcontents to leave the group after some kind of money settlement. But after numerous meetings which included Indians, state officials, and BIA personnel, the Tribal Council finally accepted the bureau draft in principle. Congressional and BIA terminationists then used the action as evidence that the Kalmaths approved of their plans.[20]

The opposition to termination, however, led by council member Boyd Jackson, struggled to change the BIA proposal when the Klamaths appeared before the joint hearings near the end of February 1953. At this point opponents felt they could not completely stop a bill and therefore tried only to maximize tribal participation and limit inducements for withrdrawal to help maintain as much group unity as possible. The Crawfords testified that the proposal did not go far enough because only total liquidation and per-capita distribution would bring the full value of the share that individuals deserved as American citizens. They scathingly attacked the communistic tribalism they hoped to eliminate. At the same time state officials expressed fears of the possible consequences of federal withdrawal on the area's economy and the fact that, in the absence of the BIA, the Indians might become dependent on Oregon. Moreover, if termination should force division of the forest, sustained-yield management as a unit would end and a denuded region would surely result.[21]

Subcommittee members conceded the possibility of excessive cutting when individual control over property ended regulations, but they insisted that personal property rights held highest priority and reported out a somewhat vague bill that authorized the tribe to hire management specialists in the preparation of plans for future supervision of tribal property. The Senate passed the bill in this form, but the House amended it to allow individual

members to withdraw and take their share of assets. This amendment would naturally force the sale of enough property to compensate those who chose to leave.[22]

Another important change gave the secretary of the interior,
rather than the tribe, the authority to select the management specialists who would hold ultimate power over planning and the
sale of land necessary to fulfill the provisions. The Senate then
concurred in the last-minute alterations, representing a victory
for those demanding complete liquidation of the reservation. A
leader of that faction, Wade Crawford, claimed credit for the success of the amendments, but several years later Oregon Senator
Richard Neuberger pointed a finger at local timber companies
eager to gain access to Indian land.[23]

The BIA also had recently tried unsuccessfully to win the approval of proposals for termination from the various tribes in
western Washington. Realizing that congressional sentiment was
against them, the Tribal Council of one of the groups, the Makah,
prepared a termination plan of its own with the help of an attorney after it found all of the bureau drafts unacceptable. Representative Jack Westland of Washington agreed to introduce it. Rather
than following the principles of conservative terminationists, the
bill adhered to the philosophy of the IRA. The Makahs would
receive a federal charter that preserved most of the governing authority of their IRA charter, but they would be removed from almost all federal or state oversight. The subcommittees considered
the proposal at the joint hearings along with the others prepared
by the BIA, but they found that it violated their termination goals.
Therefore, they did not introduce a bill.[24]

The joint subcommittees turned their attention next to a bureau-drafted proposal covering the 4212 members of Montana's
Confederated Salish and Kootenai Tribes of the Flathead Reservation. Since a high proportion of the Indians subsisted on welfare and their tribal assets did not compare with those of the
Klamaths, they seemed to be very illogical choices for quick termination. Nevertheless, proponents of federal withdrawal hoped
that deep divisions within the tribe would simplify the task of
gaining approval for the bill. The Flathead Reservation consisted
not only of peoples with different traditional affiliations, but
also included on its rolls as many members off the reservation
as on it.[25]

News that Congress was considering Flathead termination came unexpectedly to the reservation in mid-September of 1953. At that time superintendent Forest Stone told Tribal Chairman Walter McDonald that a meeting would be held in about a month to discuss the bureau bill. This was the first that McDonald had heard of the matter, and it left little opportunity for the Indians to consider a position, plan an opposition, or prepare for federal withdrawal if the legislation was successful. In the little time available, few Indians came even to a full understanding of what termination meant or would involve.[26]

The Tribal Council, representing primarily those who lived on the reservation, had unanimously rejected the proposal, and the BIA had therefore tried to ensure the participation of the outsiders, who undoubtedly would be more attracted to liquidation and a cash settlement. Officials sent circulars only to off-reservation Indians because they "had no other means of getting the information correctly." Congressmen also knew how to make a convincing case. In a meeting with a group of Flatheads, subcommittee member William Henry Harrison of Wyoming had told the Indians that their tribal assets totaled about $70,000,000 and would mean a per-capita distribution of approximately $17,000. Tribal officials insisted that the figure would be much lower, but when the story made the newspapers the amount came out even higher. Walter McDonald claimed that subcommittee members had used the alluring statistics to encourage the off-reservation Indians to petition for termination, which is exactly what happened.[27]

The BIA also used various methods to pressure the Indians into acceptance. It withdrew the Flathead land clerk, forcing the tribe to hire one at its own expense. It cut off access to Revolving Fund credit, claiming a bad collection rating. But since the service was regained almost immediately after defeat of the bill, McDonald saw it most assuredly as a matter of subtle convincing.[28]

When the opposition to the Flathead termination proposal appeared in force at the joint hearings, the room echoed in heated exchange during each of the three sessions allotted to the group. The Intertribal Policy Board, representing all seven of the Montana reservations, denounced the measure. Various witnesses expressed concerns over the expected acceleration in timber cutting once the sustained-yield management of forest units ended. D. A.

Dellwo of the Flathead Irrigation District envisioned erosion damage as non-Indian land buyers denuded the area in search of quick profits. State officials split over the effect on the local economy. Some believed that they could recover any additional service costs in new taxes on Indian property, while others felt that the poverty-stricken Flatheads might become a financial burden. Montana's congressional delegation questioned the basic assumptions of the entire policy as well as the tactics involved. Senator Mike Mansfield appealed for adherence to the treaty guarantees he still considered valid. With only two letters received by his office in favor, Representative Lee Metcalf charged terminationists with ignoring Indian opinion.[29]

At the same time, a strong opposition to Flathead termination had emerged among Montana's non-Indian citizens. Thirty-five civic, church, farm, and labor organizations had condemned the proposal at a recent state conference on social welfare. Richard Shipman of the Montana Farmers' Union appeared before the joint hearings and warned congressmen that off-reservation Native Americans would be attracted to "big money offers" and would force the sale of all the tribe's sources of income. He pointed to the BIA prediction that Montana Power Company would buy the bureau-operated Kerr dam and thus eliminate roughly $200,000 in annual tribal income derived from the sale of electricity to Montana Power.[30]

Shipman especially feared that the measure would result in additions to the state's population of landless Indians who had sold their allotments and lived in disgraceful slums on the edge of various Montana towns. He told of one such group known as the Hill 57 Indians because of the area they inhabited in Great Falls. Discussion of their condition made a sharp impression on all participants as it exemplified the fears of a huge welfare burden for the state upon termination.[31]

Subcommittee members questioned Shipman sharply, and Watkins even tried to make him appear a "stooge" of the Association on American Indian Affairs (AAIA), the group that had helped prepare his testimony. Tribal Chairman McDonald later described the Utah senator's performance as "mean." Nevertheless, the opposition was too organized and vocal, and the subcommittees dropped the Flathead termination bill from further consideration.[32]

In early March 1954 the joint subcommittees began consideration of a proposal covering about 870 Florida Seminoles. This group lived under some of the most primitive conditions of any people in America; many of them were unable to speak English and existed as they had fifty to seventy-five years earlier. Many families lived in palm-thatched houses, cooked by open campfire, and were infected by hookworms. Privies were virtually unknown, and 40 percent of the children did not attend school. A small number were relatively assimilated and made a living in nearby communities or worked on local farms during the harvest season, but the majority lived on what they could gather, hunt, or fish in the Everglades.[33]

Subcommittee members had originally included these indigent Indians on the list for quick termination in House Concurrent Resolution 108 because of the unusually high per-capita costs of the few BIA services performed in isolation from the rest of the bureau's western operations. Nonetheless, BIA officials recognized a continuing need for aid and suggested a transfer of existing services to the state if the termination bill composed by the bureau should pass. Everyone from the agency superintendent to local citizen organizations agreed that these particular Indians were totally unprepared for federal withdrawal. As a member of the Indian Affairs Subcommittee, Florida Senator George Smathers generally went along with Watkins's termination policy, but in this case he feared that unscrupulous outsiders would exploit the land and resources of these inexperienced people.[34]

With the exception of a few off-reservation members, the Indians also opposed the bill. Although unable to afford representatives at the hearings, they clearly preferred more federal aid and wanted nothing to do with the state. The Florida Seminoles were divided into two bands, Miccosukee and Muskogee. The 545 members of the extremely independent and traditional Miccosukee group even rejected congressional authority to legislate the status of their land and refused to recognize the limitations of the reservations set up a half century ago. They claimed most of the Everglades and considered themselves unconquered by the United States since they had never signed a treaty of surrender after the nineteenth-century wars. Once again the resistance to the proposed termination bill forced the subcommittee to kill the measure.[35]

The next group scheduled for hearings on a termination bill

suffered from poverty even more debilitating than that of the Seminoles. The extremely poor quality of land on the Turtle Mountain Reservation in North Dakota precluded much of the hunting and gathering that helped sustain the Florida Indians. Roughly one-half of the almost 9,000 Chippewas lived in crowded log huts with mud-filled cracks. The median annual income was only $750 and the limited work available consisted primarily of seasonal labor on large farms owned by whites. Since the sterile land remained relatively unproductive, most of the Indians relied on welfare, and thus this reservation had always been one of the most expensive to maintain. The BIA saw an accelerated relocation program before final termination as the only honorable way within budgetary constraints to relieve itself of the costly responsibilities. The legislation it proposed therefore differed slightly from the others in calling for a drastic reduction in the reservation population by helping the Indians find work in various industrial cities.[36]

Local officials and the Chippewas petitioned Congress against the plan and instead demanded massive federal aid for a reservation rehabilitation program to create an economic base for future self-sufficiency. The tribe held a boxing match to raise money for a delegation to attend the hearings in Washington. County authorities testified before the subcommittees that the area could not assume the financial burden after federal withdrawal. But Watkins rejected the protests and referred to the Chippewas as "white people masquerading under the word Indian." Generations of intermarriage since the fur traders first penetrated the northern plains centuries earlier had resulted in a significant amount of French blood in the tribe. The Utah senator apparently assumed that this made them ready for complete entrance into the dominant society. But most subcommittee members realized that these poverty-stricken Indians would make embarrassing examples for the new termination policy and therefore voted against sending a bill to the full Congress.[37]

Another very expensive part of the BIA's operation was the supervision of the over one hundred small groups scattered throughout California. The resulting costs helped make fiscally conservative terminationists receptive to that portion of the state's population that agitated for federal withdrawal. Indeed, the Mission Indian Federation had spearheaded an intense anti-BIA drive since the end of World War II. In 1950 the group's legal counselor, Purl Willis, convinced the House Appropriations Committee to drop funding for the bureau in California because it not only was unnecessary but also was used to deny Indians their "liberties." Although subsequent Senate action restored the money, California Native Americans remained among the most frequent targets of terminationists.[38]

The Mission Indian Federation favored federal withdrawal and liquidation of tribal property from an extreme right-wing, anti-IRA point of view. When the BIA proposal for the termination of California Indians came before the joint subcommittees on March 5, 1954, Purl Willis argued that the measure should go beyond the standard bureau format and authorize the immediate sale of all reservation lands and a distribution of the proceeds. He referred to former Indian Commissioner John Collier as "the voice of Russian Communists in their plans to capture the American Indian and thus start their world wide conspiracy to communize free America." The group drew much of its backing from assimilated, off-reservation Native Americans, but foes questioned its claims of support. Max Mazzeti of the Rincon Reservation charged Willis with constantly changing the number of members he purported to represent and padding the lists with duplicates and names of dead Indians. He pointed out that no tribal council in California had authorized Willis to speak for it and that most were unaware of his actions.[39]

Opponents of any change in status came primarily from the larger and more cohesive groups, especially in the southern part of the state. They considered perpetual tax exemption a fair price for the extensive land cessions of the past and saw budget cutting as the only motive for their termination. Some predicted that real-estate men would inundate their reservations after the removal of trust status and swindle them on land deals.[40]

The Indians of California, an organization which claimed to represent the state's 20,000 landless Indians, objected to the termination proposal because it ignored those who had left the unproductive reservation areas in search of employment. Some native *rancherías* had been abandoned and then occupied by members of other bands. This made it impossible in many cases to determine ownership. Instead of trying to unravel the complicated matter, the bill allowed the secretary of the interior to vest land interest in whatever tribe had occupied a plot for at least two years. Unless he could prove membership in a qualifying group, the landless Indian was excluded.[41]

As at most of the previous hearings, Watkins challenged the testimony of opponents in a hostile and contemptuous manner. In one instance, House subcommittee chairman E. Y. Berry joined the senator in a lively exchange with a relatively affluent Native American. The two tried to corner the witness into an admission that he objected to the bill only to evade taxes. In a strange twist of rhetoric borrowed from the American revolutionary period, Watkins called it representation without taxation. But the Indian insisted that he based his disapproval on more than simply monetary grounds, and once again the extensive resistance convinced the subcommittee not to report out a bill.[42]

Another early target of terminationists was the Menominee tribe of Wisconsin. By subcommittee standards this group met the criteria for federal withdrawal better than any other. In fact, BIA officials considered them already assimilated racially and otherwise. Only 75 of the 3059 members were full-blooded and their life-style revealed few trappings of an Indian heritage. The 221,696-acre tribal forest produced sufficient income for the Menominees who worked in the sawmill, as well as reimbursement to the BIA for its extensive management services.[43]

Efforts to terminate the Menominees began as early as 1947 when the bureau drew up a bill which allowed for the retention of inalienable land titles and nontaxable status for fifty years. The measure did not pass, but pressure on the tribe intensified during the years of the Truman administration under Commissioner Dillon Myer. In 1951 the Menominees won a $7,600,000 court judgment against the United States for mismanagement of their forest. But the release of the money required an act of Congress, and the BIA refused to request it without an accompanying study by the tribe of the possible transfer of supervisory responsibilities to the state or Tribal Council.[44]

The next year the Menominees submitted a plan calling for distribution of part of the money and use of the rest to improve their sawmill. Again the bureau rejected the idea without a consideration of federal withdrawal. In early 1953 the tribe sent a delegation consisting of John Fossum, Aloysius Dodge, and Gordon Dickie to Washington to present its case to Congress. At about

the same time Representative Melvin Laird of Wisconsin introduced a bill to distribute $1500 per capita from the judgment
funds. It passed the House, but Watkins held it up in the Senate
pending tribal agreement to a termination plan. The tribal delegation insisted that it could not commit the Menominees to any
such plan and suggested that Watkins visit the reservation for
discussions and to see firsthand the Indians' problems. The Utah
senator thus appeared along with various BIA officials before a
General Council meeting of all interested Menominees on June
20 and told them that their procrastination was self-destructive.
He said that Congress had decided on a policy of federal withdrawal, and they would not receive their money until they re-
lented. The Tribal Council reluctantly approved the necessary
amendment to the per-capita bill, but the measure died before
the session ended.[45]

Knowing that Watkins would bring out a BIA-drafted version
early the next year, the tribe sent the three-member delegation
to Madison, Wisconsin to explain its problems before state officials. In October the governor's Human Rights Commission expressed strong objection to the neglect of Indian opinion. The
governor then appointed a five-man committee of public officials
headed by Tax Commissioner Harry Harder to consider the state's
position.[46]

The committee had just begun its study as the 1954 congressional session opened. Even a cursory investigation clearly revealed significant difficulties in integrating the reservation into
the state's legal, educational, economic, and social order. Realizing that they had little power over the subcommittee's decisions,
state officials struggled for as much transitional time as possible.
At the request of the Menominees, Laird introduced a more mod-
erate bill to force consideration of alternatives at the hearings. It
provided for a longer period before final termination, a federal
rather than a state corporate charter to replace trusteeship, the
preservation of various treaty rights, and the extension of educational subsidies for five additional years.[47]

When the joint subcommittee met in mid-March to consider
Menominee termination, Laird complained about the lack of cooperation with the state on such an important matter. The Department of the Interior had contacted Wisconsin officials only a
short time before the hearings. State Tax Commissioner Harder

emphasized in his testimony the problems involved in such a hurried federal withdrawal. Incorporating the reservation into the area's tax structure, for example, required a forest appraisal, and the state could not appropriate funds and perform the survey within the two years specified in the BIA draft. Watkins insisted that the task of integration should not be difficult since the Menominees were practically assimilated anyway, but Harder strongly challenged the assumption that the Indians were already integrated into the surrounding community.[48]

Each subcommittee produced its own version of termination for the Menominees; the House bill conformed to Laird's less-severe measure, while the Senate supported the Watkins bill designed by the BIA. The subsequent joint conference accepted most of the Senate draft, but the House rejected it at Laird's insistence. A second conference resulted in a compromise which met the objections of the Wisconsin representative. This final version reported to the full Congress differed slightly from the Bureau's standard format. While it accomplished the goal of terminating federal supervision and trusteeship status, it avoided any liquidation of the reservation. With the help of the BIA and outside specialists, the Menominees were to submit plans for the future control of tribal property and economic organization by December 31, 1957. One year later title to the land would revert to the tribe.[49]

The joint subcommittee's last hearing in mid-April of 1954 involved seven small bands of Shoshones and Paiutes in Nevada: Ruby Valley, Yerington, Battle Mountain, Carson, Las Vegas, Lovelock, and Reno-Sparks. These groups had not been listed in House Concurrent Resolution 108, but the BIA prepared a termination bill at the request of Nevada Representative Clifton Young. Their indigence compared with that of the poorest groups previously considered. Although some of the reservations lay partly within the city limits of various towns, the Indians lacked such basic facilities as sewer lines, water systems, roads, and adequate housing. Many of the groups owed the BIA large sums of money for the construction of irrigation projects.

In some cases, not confined only to Nevada, the BIA constructed irrigation projects on reservations, charged certain "reimbursable" costs to Indians, and then loaned them money or cattle to get started. Many failed and went deeply into debt, sometimes largely because they had too little acreage or too few cattle to constitute a self-sustaining operation. Native Americans did not share in any of the decision-making, including the original decision to build a project. Like all the other proposed bills, this one required the repayment of debts, and the money could only come from the sale of land after termination since the Indians had few other assets.[50]

None of the Shoshones or Paiutes could afford to send delegates to the hearings, but tribal representatives wrote to the subcommittees and pleaded for a cancellation of the debts and for federal grants to construct essential service facilities before withdrawal. Local officials naturally dreaded the prospect of being left with responsibility for the poverty-stricken Indians and also testified in favor of an aid program. Representative Young curtly responded to that idea with the question: "How far do you think the American taxpayer should go in doing that to discharge our responsibilities to our Indian citizens?" Because of the resistance and controversy concerning these Native Americans, the subcommittees did not recommend a termination bill to the full Congress.[51]

Even before they ended, the hearings raised numerous questions concerning the procedures and the soundness, morality, and motives of the termination policy. In February 1954 the *Minot Daily News* carried a series of emotional articles which described the poverty of the Turtle Mountain Reservation Indians and their bitterness over termination. The articles soon reached an audience far beyond the northern plains after congressmen had them reprinted in various government publications. Former Indian commissioner John Collier charged that private economic interests eager to grab Indian land had actually promoted the bills. AAIA president Oliver La Farge agreed that the discovery of oil in Utah had played a role in the Paiute case and accused the BIA of abdicating its responsibilities toward Native Americans. When asked to comment on La Farge's allegations, Emmons replied that he was under congressional mandate and had to draw up the bills.[52]

Near the end of February a group of social scientists under the sponsorship of the Wenner-Gren Foundation for Anthropological Research met at the University of Chicago to examine and discuss the controversial new policy. Their subsequent report not only criticized recent actions but also challenged the underlying assumption that integration was inevitable and desirable. At about the same time Joseph Garry, a Coeur d'Alene Indian and Idaho state representative, organized a meeting in Washington sponsored by the National Congress of American Indians (NCAI) to consolidate Indian opposition.[53]

After encountering increasingly stiff resistance both inside and outside of the hearings, the 1954 drive for termination achieved only limited success. Congress first passed the Menominee bill on June 17, followed in mid-August by measures covering the western Oregon bands, the Klamaths, the four bands of Utah Paiutes, and the Alabama-Coushattas. Although opponents urged presidential vetoes, Eisenhower signed all of them.[54]

At the same time Congress passed a termination bill involving two factions on Utah's Uintah and Ouray Reservation that was not included in either House Concurrent Resolution 108 or the joint hearings. The tribe consisted of a majority of very traditional full bloods and a smaller group of partially assimilated mixed bloods. A recent $19,000,000 judgment won against the United States in the U.S. Court of Claims made them likely candidates for a major rehabilitation project since it could be done without government expense. The arrangements in this bill amounted to a combination of termination and rehabilitation on terms acceptable to a budget-minded administration. After a division of assets, the mixed bloods would undergo a phased withdrawal over a seven-year period. Meanwhile, the BIA would supervise a special development program for the full bloods with a goal of termination in twenty-five years. Emmons boasted that the tribe instigated the move and formulated most of the plan. But some members claimed that a handful of more successful mixed-blood ranchers had initiated the action after pressure from the tribal attorney and the BIA superintendent. Bureau authority to approve attorney contracts with tribes helped ensure that the attorneys would work closely with the BIA. If they stepped out of line and defended Indian positions too vigorously, Congress and the bureau became alarmed and tried to remove them. Certainly some unethical conduct by lawyers warranted official investigation and action, but the power over attorney contracts also was used to guarantee that lawyers not encourage Native Americans to become unmanageable.[55]

Judging from the tribes chosen for early legislative action, terminationists placed highest priority on cost cutting and on setting policy-reversing precedents by starting with the easiest and least complex cases. Both criteria actually worked against full success in 1954 as well as in the long term. The most expensive groups to maintain and those receiving the fewest services to complicate implementation were inevitably some of the most impoverished and needy. The specter of abandonment stimulated the loudest protest and damaged the credibility of the "liberation" rhetoric.

Of the few bills passed, most involved small, disorganized groups with minor assets and with enough members favorable to termination to allow claims of tribal acceptance. The Menominee and Klamath measures were exceptions. Terminationists who believed these comparatively affluent and assimilated Indians were the most ready had promoted legislation affecting them with special vigor in hopes that they would serve as models for future action.[56]

# 5

# Withdrawal by Attrition

While legislative action to drop certain tribes from federal supervision proceeded, terminationists also began escalating efforts to dismantle the BIA by slowly eliminating various functions. For a year and a half this type of federal withdrawal advanced at an unprecedented pace. The subcommittees and the bureau implemented the Bimson Report wherever possible, cutting costs and assimilating Indians into service facilities outside the BIA.

Emmons's first move involved the funds coming into the hands of some tribes from Claims Commission settlements or from the increasing income from petroleum, mineral, and agricultural leases. Normally such money went to the United States Treasury in trust for Indians. The former banker hoped to encourage the use of private institutions to hold these funds as the government shed its trust responsibilities. While attending the New York Midwinter Trust Conference in February 1954, he tried to interest the financial community in the investment possibilities of Indian money. He convinced old American Banker's Association (ABA) friends to help create a special informal committee to work toward his goal. Three members of the ABA's trust division agreed to take part. Richard G. Stockton was chairman of the board of the Wachovia Bank and Trust Company in Winston-Salem, North Carolina. John W. Remington headed the Lincoln-Rochester Trust Company of Rochester, New York. And Edwin P. Neilan served as executive vice-president of the Equitable Security Trust Company of Wilmington, Delaware.[1]

At about the same time, Emmons initiated limited moves toward reservation rehabilitation and development. Unlike a few of the more extreme western conservatives, he did not favor immediate termination for all groups. Some required help in advancing to the point where they could be assimilated. He also realized

49

the necessity of addressing native expectations of federal aid, especially since the Navajo-Hopi Act of 1950. But budgetary restraints relegated reservation rehabilitation to a very low priority. Nonetheless, Emmons and the bureau vigorously advertised a "three-prong attack" to deal with the most basic needs on reservations. In news releases and speeches across the nation, Emmons emphasized a BIA commitment to improve health, education, and economic opportunity. Newspapers reported it as a new aid program. The Washington *Daily News* even called it a "Point Four at Home."[2]

The fanfare was intended in part to defuse criticism and ease Indian apprehension over the new termination policy. It certainly created a distorted image of the effort. The administration goal of reduced government activity and limited spending severely restricted the program and defined its nature. For example, Emmons's first moves toward stimulating reservation economic development were unhurried, involved no direct BIA role, and also fitted into the prevailing conservative ideology. Rather than create tribal enterprises, Emmons worked toward incorporating Indians into existing industrial and commercial networks.

Tribal enterprises had never received significant support. John Collier had tried promoting them while serving as commissioner in the 1930s but always with limited funding. Nevertheless, Emmons believed that past experience showed they would not work. The reason he gave was the difficulty they experienced in finding adequate markets. BIA policy throughout the 1950s also revealed a lack of faith in the capabilities of Native Americans to manage their own businesses.[3]

Studies of available resources on reservations were a prerequisite to any plan of action. Armed with information on areas of potential business expansion, Emmons hoped industrialists would be interested enough to locate factories on or near reservations. He could point to numerous undeveloped natural resources, such as timber, oil, gas, and minerals, plus an unlimited supply of cheap labor. The commissioner had approached the Rockefeller Foundation in hopes it would fund the surveys, but it would not donate to anything immediately related to the formulation of government policy.[4]

Emmons then enlisted the aid of business friends. He envisioned a private organization that would solicit grants from large foundations to finance the resource studies. David Thomas Beals agreed to head the effort. His experience ensured wide contacts in the business community; he had served as chairman of the board of Kansas City's First National Bank, president of the Interstate Cattle Loan Company, and director of the Crowe Coal Company. New York attorney and former undersecretary of the treasury Roswell Magill became the second member, adding legal and financial expertise. A short while later the addition of Harvard anthropologist Clyde Kluckhohn gave the group a prominent intellectual. Activities moved very slowly at first. Everyone involved could devote only part of his time to the effort, so they experienced difficulty arranging meetings and completing the procedures necessary for the group's incorporation. They tried to find someone to lead the drive fulltime but lacked the money to pay a salary.[5]

Similarly, the only significant new undertaking in education came on the Navajo Reservation, where a year before Emmons had garnered his only tribal endorsement for commissioner. And even there the effort involved little increased expenditure and was well within the admittedly inadequate spending projection of the 1950 Long Range Act. A BIA study shortly after World War II found that 68 percent of Navajos had no schooling and 88 percent of young men were illiterate. It estimated that $90 million would be required to bring 75 percent of school-age children into the classroom. The Long Range Act earmarked $25 million to accommodate 55 percent and incorrectly assumed that since BIA estimates had concluded that the reservation could support only 35,000 people, the relocation program would eliminate the need to make room for the rest.[6]

For the first few years a tightfisted Congress kept actual construction expenditures under the act so low that progress could not outpace the population increase. The Tribal Council became deeply concerned and in March 1954 endorsed the Bimson Report's recommendation to alter construction plans to accommodate more students with less money. Emmons subsequently created the Navajo Emergency Education Program (NEEP) and stopped "trying to build mansions out there for every schoolhouse." The BIA cut about $4.5 million from scheduled construction and reprogrammed it for more intensive use of space. Many new building projects were eliminated and steps taken to economize on the

rest. In existing facilities officials converted dining and recreational areas into classrooms or dormitories at boarding schools.
Quonset huts replaced the dormitories freed for instruction. The
bureau also increased from six to thirty-six the fleet of mobile
trailer schools that served the children of nomadic sheepherders
and sent more young Navajos to the various off-reservation BIA
facilities. All of this resulted in facilities that one specialist in
the education branch referred to as "woefully substandard," but
since buildings represented only one aspect in determining the
quality of education, the same official concluded that the important precedent of universal education as quickly as possible
outweighed any deficiencies in physical structures.[7]

NEEP also included a Bordertown Dormitory Program that
helped bring more students into the classroom. The bureau contracted with school districts in Aztec and Gallup, New Mexico;
Holbrook, Winslow, and Snowflake, Arizona; and Richfield, Utah
to enroll Navajos into their systems. The BIA retained responsibility for dormitory facilities and at first used such makeshift
quarters as bowling alleys and tourist courts. In separate agreements with state departments of public instruction, the bureau
accepted the full costs of educating the students. In addition, local
districts received $1,000 per pupil to pay for new classroom space.[8]

By enrolling more Indian children in public schools, the Bordertown Dormitory Program also reflected new BIA objectives in Indian education. Although much of the groundwork had been laid
by the administration of Commissioner Charles Rhoads beginning in 1928, John Collier's education director, Willard Walcott
Beatty, was largely responsible for utilizing ideas of progressive
education inspired by John Dewey and of recent anthropological
concepts of cultural relativity. He emphasized, for example, community schooling to make educational institutions centers of
local cultural life, directed course work toward the economic
needs of individual reservations, and introduced aspects of Indian
culture into curricula. However, Emmons's educational director,
Hildegard Thompson, altered that fundamental policy to match
larger bureau goals by reducing the emphasis on community
schooling and instituting programs designed to assimilate Indian
children culturally into the dominant social system and to prepare them for jobs within an urban, technological society. Mix-
ing Native Americans with whites in public schools was seen as

one way of achieving such integration, and this effort continued throughout Emmons's term in office.[9]

Emmons thought he could get the necessary additional $3 million from the Department of Health, Education, and Welfare (HEW) under Public Law 815, which subsidized public school construction in areas impacted by nontaxable federal facilities. When that proved impossible, he pleaded before a House subcommittee for supplemental funds under the Long Range Act. This was the first meeting between the budget-conscious appropriations subcommittee that controlled BIA expenditures and the new commissioner, who considered himself "just a country boy," still unfamiliar with the complicated bureaucracy in Washington, D.C. Colleagues had warned Emmons that it would be tough, but a couple of personal connections made the experience fairly comfortable and in the commissioner's mind helped win the money despite the subcommittee's reluctance to set any precedents that might encourage more requests. Administration support for the scheme was gained largely through the influence of Budget Director Joseph Dodge, whose friendship with Emmons dated from the time Dodge was the president of Detroit Bank and both played leadership roles in the American Banker's Association. In the House subcommittee, chairman Ben Jensen of Iowa remembered Emmons's 1944 run for the governorship of New Mexico when his brother Neal Jensen headed the Emmons for Governor Committee. He treated the commissioner like an old friend but refused to go along at first. Jensen finally conceded when the chairman of the Senate Appropriations Subcommittee, Republican Guy Cordan of Oregon, worked for passage, undoubtedly at the insistence of Arthur Watkins, who realized the importance of such moves to his own plans for termination. The 8,000 additional Navajos attending school that fall under the BIA's only expansion program, together with smaller increases in subsequent years, certainly represented a noteworthy accomplishment. In the bureau's campaign to publicize the government attack on reservation problems, however, these examples of progress became overworked.[10]

The last part of the "three-prong attack" was transferred out of BIA jurisdiction before the bureau could undertake any significant improvements. Health facilities for Indians had failed to keep pace with modern medical standards over the years. Native

American death rates from measles were still twenty times the national average, from pneumonia and influenza four times, and from tuberculosis nine times. Underfunding contributed to the problem. Orme Lewis, the assistant interior secretary, later noted that "it was horrendously difficult to get an appropriation for the Bureau that included enough money for Health." The BIA's difficulty in attracting doctors also played a role. Bureau physicians not only received low salaries but also worked in isolation away from modern facilities, teaching programs, and living quarters. In recent years over half of them came to the BIA on loan after being drafted into HEW's Public Health Service (PHS). As Korean War draft calls fell, PHS could no longer transfer personnel away.[11]

The bureau had periodically closed its smaller hospitals and contracted with state, local, or private health facilities to care for Native Americans. The primary purpose of the action was to reduce costs since small government units had higher per-patient overhead, but it also reduced the need for BIA doctors. The affected Indians frequently protested, however, because the change usually meant greater distance to a hospital and personnel who understood them less, discriminated more, and who could not devote their full attention to the Indians' care.[12]

Congressional terminationists had failed in attempts to transfer all BIA health responsibilities to PHS in 1953, largely because of bureau protests, but a year later Emmons followed the Bimson Report's recommendation and actively promoted the scheme. The National Congress of American Indians (NCAI) agreed that the move would mean better care and therefore approved. But for some Indians the notion raised all of the fears of previous transfers by contract. The Oklahoma congressional delegation fought hard against the measure, contending that the native citizens it served almost unanimously objected. Senator John Stennis of Mississippi, whose constituency included some Choctaws in his state, tacked on an amendment forbidding any hospital closings without consent, but the conference committee later struck it out.[13]

Opposition also came from HEW, which gave as its reason the concern previously expressed by the BIA over breaking up a unified program covering all Indian affairs. In addition, it dreaded taking on such a monumental task. The cost-conscious Bureau of the Budget disapproved because it felt that wasteful inefficiency would result from the fragmentation. With opinion split within as well as outside of the administration, the active support of Watkins, chairman of the Senate Indian Affairs Subcommittee, undoubtedly made the difference. The bill as passed in August 1954 set July 1, 1955 as the effective date. PHS did receive higher appropriations for the task thereafter, and improvements in Indian health resulted over the next decade. But the transfer also meant the closing of some small BIA hospitals in remote regions, and the affected Indians, who sometimes had to travel over one hundred miles to the nearest PHS facility, protested whenever they found the opportunity.[14]

Recent debates over controversial policies only escalated the opposition already growing out of reaction against termination legislation and Public Law 280. Indians slowly became more politically effective at making their voices heard. In another attempt at a transfer bill within the terminationists' legislative package, Senator Watkins and Barry Goldwater of Arizona introduced a measure that same summer to shift BIA agricultural extension activities to the Department of Agriculture. Assistant Secretary of the Interior Orme Lewis argued that the Department of Agriculture was better equipped to carry on the service. Secretary of Agriculture Ezra Benson and the director of the Bureau of the Budget also approved of the proposal.[15]

Although opinion in the Native American community was split, those not in favor agitated so effectively that some congressmen from Indian-populated districts came out against the move. The Navajo Tribal Council approved, but the powerful All-Pueblo Council joined smaller groups throughout the West in opposition. New Mexico Senator Clinton Anderson had supported even the most controversial bills of the past few years but testified at subcommittee hearings against this one. He articulated the Indian fears that Department of Agriculture personnel would not understand the language and the cultural differences that BIA agents had grown accustomed to. He also predicted that without an interest in the whole Indian program, the Department of Agriculture would not fight hard to win adequate extension service appropriations from Congress. The measure made it out of the Senate only after Dennis Chavez of New Mexico amended it to exclude Indians in his state as well as those in neighboring Arizona. Once the bill was in the House, the Committee on Interior and Insular Affairs reported it out favorably, but when proponents tried the usual tactic of passage on the consent calendar, several representatives led by Montana's Lee Metcalf protested the lack of tribal consent and killed the bill.[16]

By this time Representative Metcalf was quickly becoming the foremost agitator in the House against the whole tenor of Indian policy under the Eisenhower administration. In another important action he rekindled the sharp debate over "consent or consultation" that had erupted a year earlier after passage of Public Law 280. The liberal Democrat promptly followed the president's suggestion and introduced an amendment providing for tribal consent before any state takeover of law-and-order jurisdiction. Largely because of the influence of Watkins, the proposal received no attention in either subcommittee on Indian affairs. Watkins acknowledged substantial pressure to alter the law but wrote to Eisenhower and strongly urged the administration not to support the amendment it had called for the previous year. He realized that the debate went to the very heart of his termination plans and that if "the choice [was] consent, the U.S. [would] forever be saddled with trust relationship, allowing those who are greedy and well-educated to take advantage of tax exemption." A similar bill made it past Watkins a year later and was favorably reported by the Senate Committee on Interior and Insular Affairs, but the House subcommittee rejected it.[17]

Meanwhile, the BIA worked on the Bimson Report's recommendations on economizing and reducing bureau activities. Emmons appointed Leon V. Langan, assistant to the commissioner and former manager of the Gallup Chamber of Commerce, to direct the effort. The Bimson team, for example, had concluded that moving Indians into urban areas would be cheaper over the long term than continuing to maintain services on reservations. Even under former commissioner Dillon Myer, the BIA had realized this and tried to gain more funding for an expansion of its relocation program. But parsimonious appropriations committees refused to allow large increases for any project, so granted only modest raises. Emmons experienced the same when he requested more money. The bureau subsequently stretched the available dollar as far as possible and opened the way for attacks by creating conditions ripe for criticism.[18]

When Emmons came to office, the relocation program had

helped move about twenty-six hundred Native Americans annually to Chicago, Los Angeles, Denver, or Salt Lake City. From the BIA's overworked and undermanned staff, most received minimal aid in finding a job, plus counseling and assistance in the physical and cultural transition. Much of the assistance involved such basics as finding a place to live, using telephones, opening checking accounts, and reading city maps. About 25 percent of the least affluent also received material help, including funds to cover the costs of transporting an individual's family and household goods or subsistence money until a job could be found. The only employment available to unskilled relocatees was at the bottom of the wage scale. Housing naturally had to fit within BIA resources and Indian incomes, and that invariably meant lower-class neighborhoods.[19]

Emmons repeatedly emphasized the voluntary nature of the program, but slick, high-pressure advertising, combined with a lack of alternatives, often made the choice to relocate an inevitable one. Indians learned of the program either from a BIA relocation officer or from one of many pamphlets distributed in trading stores or other common meeting places. Both sources contrasted reservation conditions with the material benefits of urban affluence. Pictures of contented Indian men working at good jobs and of women beside televisions or refrigerators were the most common tactics.[20]

The hope for employment and abundance was often overwhelmingly enticing. One former BIA official at the Winnebago agency later revealed much about the vulnerability of the poor to bureau recruiting tactics; he noted that "everyone was jumping on the bandwagon" when bureau employees rounded people up in trucks and simply asked them if they wanted "to go to California or somewhere to get a job."[21]

The bureau contended that it put applicants through a careful selection process, but recruiters reaching for quotas frequently sent Indians with very little education, limited ability to speak English, or innumerable other deficiencies that almost guaranteed failure in an alien city. The bureau also insisted that Native Americans relocated in order to find steady employment; they had the same desire for upward mobility that drove other Americans. But that motive was often compounded by a need to escape the many personal and family problems that result from poverty. Many undoubtedly went for the same reason as the niece of Harry Belvin, a prominent Choctaw leader. When her husband lost his job and a loan could not be obtained, the couple and their six children applied for relocation.[22]

The number of relocatees returning to reservations was always a problem and a matter of controversy. The BIA established policies to discourage returns, such as moving Indians to cities farthest from their homes. It also sometimes refused to give out names and addresses of other nearby Native Americans since association would encourage Indian cultural contacts and identification rather than assimilation and would perhaps promote nostalgic talk of home. The bureau claimed that only 30 percent of relocatees ever returned to reservations, but critics contended that the number was much higher. The U.S. comptroller general attacked the BIA for not keeping adequate statistics, so the correct figure could be determined, and in response, the bureau ceased the collection of data altogether, maintaining that it only provided critics with ammunition.[23]

Of those Indians who stayed in cities, certainly some found good jobs and successfully adjusted to urban life. But no one knew how many melted into the cultural no-man's-land of America's inner-city slums. There were immense problems to overcome. Economics played a big part. If a relocatee lost his job, finding another could be difficult. Sometimes the promised employment did not materialize after moving. One Sioux from Pine Ridge, South Dakota could find only temporary work in Denver rather than the position he was led to expect, and he finally returned home after weeks of walking the streets in search of a job. Racial discrimination was also an obstacle. Oliver Eastman, a Wahpeton Sioux who, atypically, was a union carpenter, found that in California ethnic groups such as Italians and Arkies (refugees from the Arkansas dust bowl in the 1930s) were given preference over Indians and Mexicans.[24]

Perhaps the greatest problem was simply the overwhelming cultural dislocation. Strong family and community ties naturally made some homesick. Many could not adjust to urban life. A former relocation officer state it succinctly when he described the difficulty experienced by an Indian who "has never been permanently employed, has never looked at a clock, and is expected with a weeks counseling or three weeks counseling to go out and face the world."[25]

The BIA had also learned to reduce its expenditures and phase itself out of existence by transferring various functions under authority of the 1934 Johnson-O'Malley Act. Near the end of Dillon Myer's term, for example, the BIA began negotiating with states and counties for their assumption of road maintenance on reservations. The project involved a massive rehabilitation program since communities would not accept roads unless they met local construction standards. Emmons immediately accelerated this process, and despite another funding struggle with appropriations committees, he increased the number of miles transferred by over threefold in fiscal 1954. The passage that same year of the Federal Highway Act eased the problem of inadequate financing somewhat because it included specific provisions for reservation roads. The costs could then be authorized under other auspices than an agency that the Congress deemed destined for extinction. The road transfer program thus continued and enjoyed more success than most others.[26]

The commissioner also hastened the same process in agricultural extension work, especially after the failure of the Watkins and Goldwater transfer bill. By contracting with states and counties to serve specific reservations, the bureau could achieve through administration what terminationists could not win through legislation. The first contract after Congress dropped the issue came in the fall of 1954. The BIA negotiated with Plata and Montezuma counties in Colorado to work on the Southern and Mountain Ute reservations respectively. Each tribe contributed $3,600 to pay for the services. The bureau added $5,400, and the state matched the sum of those figures, bringing the total to $25,200. The contract called for a home demonstration agent and an extension agent for each group, but it soon required renegotiation because of disagreement over the length of time personnel were to spend with Native Americans. Even more serious Indian dissatisfaction resulted, owing to different instruction techniques and a lack of understanding by county officials of cultural differences in dealing with natives.[27]

Another way of reducing costs and activities was to remove Indian land from trust or restricted status and thus eliminate the expenses involved in heirship probating and the supervision of leases. Under existing law the BIA was required to divide the interest in trust property among the descendents of the original allotment owner. After several generations the number of people with an interest in even small plots of land sometimes reached ridiculous proportions. It was not unusual for an Indian to own a fraction like 33/10,000 of an allotment. Such complex entanglements discouraged either tribal or individual Indian use of the land, and much of it was therefore leased to non-Indians because it was easier to divide the earnings. Checks for only a few cents were not uncommon.[28]

But this type of action opened the way for sales, and since tribes and individual Native Americans usually lacked money to buy the property, white westerners eager to exploit Indian resources naturally bought it. These sales exacerbated the problem of a dwindling land base and left checkerboard reservations with holdings of Indians and whites so intermingled that the land became useless for tribal enterprise. After commissioner Collier ended further allotment and extended trusts indefinitely in the 1930s, Native Americans could no longer get trust status removed and obtain a fee-patent title. Beginning in 1947 the BIA again changed the policy and issued fee patents with bureau approval if the allotment was not part of a timber or grazing unit benefiting the whole tribe. At the beginning of Emmons's term, after Congress failed to pass the Competency Bill which would have automatically ended trust status when an Indian reached age twenty-one, the commissioner made efforts to fee patent as much land as possible administratively.[29]

During fiscal 1954 Emmons more than doubled the number of fee patents approved by the BIA. In the spring of that year he issued the infamous "All or None" regulation. When an Indian filed for a status change, he was required to include all of his land, not just a portion of it. In addition, sales of trust property between Indians were no longer allowed, and Native Americans thereafter had to obtain a fee patent before any such transaction. An even more controversial move came on May 16, 1955, when the commissioner altered the policy on approving fee patents according to instructions from the assistant secretary of the interior, Orme Lewis. The bureau began to consider personal interest over group interest in deciding an application. Emmons acknowledged the potential harm to a reservation's livelihood, but insisted that it was his responsibility as trustee to look out for the individual. The same reasoning justified another regulation governing land sales supervised by the BIA. Rather than give Indians the first opportunity to buy advertised property or to meet the highest offer, the top bid took the sale. Whites could usually outprice Native Americans, but Emmons contended that any departure from totally competitive bidding unfairly depressed prices.[30]

Several months later the subcommittees came up with a way to achieve the results of the Competency Bill for at least some Indian lands. The Department of Interior's solicitor had found that proposal to be unconstitutional because the forced fee patenting of trust lands without Indian consent violated the Dawes Act provision that upon removal of trust status Indians would receive their property "free of all charge or encumbrances whatsoever." The Supreme Court had declared that this provision constituted a vested right against taxation. But allotment on the Cherokee, Choctaw, Chickasaw, Seminole, and Creek reservations in Oklahoma had come under the Curtis Act of 1898 and the Burke Act of 1906 rather than under the Dawes Act, and those laws did not include the terminology that prevented imposed fee patenting. Thus, Congress enacted a bill that allowed the secretary of the interior to remove restrictions on the allotments of the Five Civilized Tribes without prior application.[31]

At the same time, Congress passed a measure which accomplished through liberalized leasing one of the main objectives of the drive to eliminate trust status. Barry Goldwater introduced a proposal to extend the allowable uses of leased Indian land in Arizona beyond agriculture, grazing, and mining to include also public, religious, educational, recreational, or business purposes. The subcommittees turned it into a bill of general application and increased the length of leases from five to ten years for grazing and from ten to twenty-five years for all others. This facilitated more advanced types of economic development by non-Indians and thus expanded the possibilities of business enterprise on reservations. Proponents stressed the added income to tribes from permits and over the next few years often pointed to the Aguas Calientes, who leased land in the luxurious tourist district in Palm Springs, California. But they ignored the broader implications for the cultural, social, and political future of Native Americans. The increase in business leases would also bring many non-Indians onto reservations, often in important positions affecting a tribe's development and decision-making process.[32]

The BIA also attempted to cut its budget and activities by trying to bring greater cost effectiveness to its operations. Emmons and the Bimson team that had created the guidelines for the early years of the new administration believed that private business performed much more efficiently than government. If facilities managed by tribes or the bureau were not self-sustaining, competed with private companies, or could be obtained for less money elsewhere, the BIA closed or sold them or turned the services over to private businesses by contract. Throughout 1954 and 1955 the changes affected dairies, laundries, garages, farms, and telephone and power systems. Even in bureau schools, laundering and food services that had been performed by BIA employees and student help were turned over to outside organizations.[33]

On the Cherokee Reservation in North Carolina, for example, the bureau entered into a negotiated agreement with Cleaves Food Service of Silver Spring, Maryland, headed by Ward Cleaves, an Interior Department consultant and former army colonel, to take over food services for about 800 school children. In another move, the BIA began renting cars from a Baltimore firm for the use of top-level administrators rather than having them drive regular government vehicles. But after congressional and public criticism, including charges of rigged contracts, the bureau put the food concession up for competitive bidding and cancelled the auto agreement.[34]

In some cases the policy affected the economies and social configuration of Indian communities. The BIA usually had performed the various types of construction jobs on reservations and hired Native Americans for much of the labor force. But under Emmons it began to contract with private companies that supplied their own workers, and Indians thus lost employment. In Alaska BIA personnel doubted the ability of Indian cooperative fish canneries to succeed and tried to interest non-Indian companies in leasing the facilities or buying them out. In 1954 G. P. Halferty, Inc., and Oceanic Fisheries, Inc., leased a plant formerly operated by the Klawok Community Association. Shortly thereafter, Whiz Fish Products took over the cannery at Kake, Alaska. Since the BIA held loans on the Indian cooperatives and recent salmon runs had been poor, officials did not hesitate to do whatever necessary to avoid losses to the agency. They attached the wages of association members and workers, arbitrarily repossessed fishing boats, and pressured Indian canneries to close by threatening not to refinance the loans if profits were not forthcoming. A congressional investigation several years later condemned the strict profit-and-loss approach and charged that the bypassing of Indian leadership disregarded the intent of IRA Revolving Fund loans by discouraging Indian participation and self-control.[35]

Carrying out recent termination legislation also slightly reduced BIA responsibilities. The small bands in western Oregon and Utah, for example, chose to sell most of their lands formerly held in trust.[36] But in the most complex cases, the bureau's haste, economizing, and avoidance of the tribal leaders contributed to Indian opposition; furthermore, inherent problems in the bills made implementation unworkable and the transition period full of confrontation and controversy.

In early 1955 Interior Secretary McKay selected the three management specialists who were to be responsible for property appraisals, elections to determine the number of withdrawals, decisions over sales of group holdings, and future management reports on the Klamath Reservation. He filled the $1,000-per-month positions with old political and personal friends. T. B. Watters had thirty years of experience in real estate and insurance and formerly had served as Klamath Falls mayor and Klamath County Republican treasurer. Eugene G. Favell also worked in real estate, having specialized for the past forty years in timberland and lumber brokerage. W. L. Phillips owned the Ford automobile agency in Salem, Oregon that used to compete with McKay's General Motors car business and had managed the secretary's election to the Oregon governorship in 1948. Although they had no power over the appointments, the Indians voted them down in General Council but later were convinced to reverse their votes.[37]

In early July McKay ordered elections to pick the three-man advisory committee to work with the management specialists. The badly torn tribe chose two members who favored liquidation and one who represented those opposed to termination altogether. Most Klamaths lacked confidence that a viable tribal body could survive and also deeply mistrusted the BIA, which they believed had recently overharvested their valuable virgin timber. Although some genuinely wanted reservation dismemberment, many others cast a vote for proliquidation candidates so they could get out while their forest would still bring a good price.[38]

From the beginning the two groups did not get along. Throughout 1955 the management specialists contracted with research and survey companies, and as reports came in, they concluded that implementation would be disastrous. The Indian advisory committee pushed for liquidation and resented its lack of authority and the high salaries and expense accounts coming out of tribal funds for men they disagreed with so strongly. The Indians were also supposed to be reimbursed for expenses, but in the fall the secretary of the interior rejected their budget because it did not conform to prescribed procedures, and thus virtually put them out of business. He later dissolved the committee completely.[39]

On the Menominee Reservation the BIA's rush to leave led to near chaos in planning for the change. In early 1955 the bureau cut its staff on the reservation by 50 percent and began transferring various management responsibilities to the Advisory Council, a body which governed the tribe between meetings of the all-inclusive General Council. The bureau also reduced appropriations for reservation services, forcing the Advisory Council to begin charging fees, and rejected a Menominee request for a relocation officer. The University of Wisconsin agreed to conduct a series of studies on a wide range of topics involving the transition. The state created a Menominee Indian Study Committee chaired by the attorney general, which also included state senators and assemblymen from counties adjoining the reservation, members of neighboring county boards of commissioners, three Menominees, and representatives of various state agencies. But both efforts had only an indirect effect on the planning; the assumption was that the Indians would take the primary initiative.[40]

Tribal government, however, had never functioned well because only a few families participated while the rest remained apathetic. Traditional divisions deepened when the tribe was suddenly handed significant decision-making responsibilities, and disagreement prevented action. Moreover, as Menominees grew increasingly bitter over reductions in funding and the lack of assistance from the BIA in termination planning, they withheld cooperation. When officials discovered underpayments in recent per-capita distributions of tribal income, Emmons strongly urged the Indians to keep the $2.5 million with the tribe. The sawmill would soon stand alone as the only economic base for the group, which would need the cash to strengthen its precarious position. In referendum, however, the tribe defied the commissioner and voted to distribute the money.[41]

# Opposition Intensifies

The BIA's handling of terminated groups aggravated doubts over the policy generated at the hearings by the haste and disregard of Native American opinion. Opposition forces had stirred enough controversy and accumulated enough support by mid-1955 to slow the momentum toward federal withdrawal and to affect the direction of Indian policy.[1]

Termination planning met increasingly formidable resistance. The BIA, for example, hoped to win a bill covering some California reservations by substituting a selective measure for the previously unsuccessful all-inclusive proposal. But support for any termination bill was fading. A group of California Native Americans opposed to federal withdrawal had recently formed the California Indian Congress headed by a Pitt River Indian, Erin Forest. Representatives from about forty tribes demonstrated in Sacramento in 1955 and demanded the right of consent before any change in status. Even the state, which had favored the move earlier, grew disinclined after a study by its senate had confirmed the fears of some officials that it might heap unwanted economic and social burdens on California and its localities.[2]

On the Fort Berthold Reservation in North Dakota, Indians had recently been granted $1.5 million for lands condemned by the government to construct flood-control projects on the upper Missouri River. The BIA had withheld approval of any distribution of the money until the tribe agreed on a termination plan. But by this time there was little hope for a bill. Poverty conditions on the Fort Berthold Reservation too closely resembled the embarrassing distress of some of the groups included in the ill-fated termination attempts of the previous year. A tribal delegation therefore convinced the commissioner to relent and to recommend that the Indian affairs subcommittees release the funds without forcing the loss of trusteeship and federal services.[3]

In southern Minnesota the BIA had been reducing federal services to the various small Sioux tribes for the past several years. After his Native American constituents became targets in bureau termination planning, Senator Hubert Humphrey demonstrated that he would fight any such move. The Minnesota Democrat attacked recent cuts affecting Indians and joined the state's House delegation in submitting a proposal of its own. The bill called for a Minnesota Indian Administration with a $10 million working fund to stimulate reservation economies and for a plan for federal withdrawal to occur after at least eight years. The subcommittees found the measure unacceptable and gave it no attention.[4]

Recent changes liberalizing sales of Indian land had aroused the most severe criticism of all the administration's policies. The National Congress of American Indians (NCAI), the Association on American Indian Affairs (AAIA), the Indian Rights Association, and the Friends Committee on National Legislation had joined together in a statement of opposition shortly after the issuance of the controversial May 16 memorandum that had placed individual over tribal interests in the consideration of a request for a fee patent on a trust allotment.[5]

When the NCAI held its twelfth annual convention in the late summer of 1955, the attacks became even more intense. Numerous speakers denounced new land policies, and the assembly passed a resolution requesting that Congress appropriate funds for tribal land purchases to increase Indian holdings. Emmons defended the administration's actions before the group and tried to reassure his audience that there would "not be a dissolution of the tribes." However, in a small concession to critics of the May 16 ruling, he also announced the formation of a special board to share with the BIA the authority to make land sales decisions.[6]

A short time later AAIA president Oliver La Farge charged in a letter to the White House that the administration's policies were an attempt to, among other things, disperse Indian communities. He called BIA consultations with tribes a mockery and described widespread anxiety and disappointment on the nation's reservations. Secretary of the Interior McKay retaliated to La Farge's well-publicized accusations with a lengthy rebuttal issued to the press.[7]

As the controversy mounted, various church groups began a massive project in 1955 to inform members about recent issues in

Indian affairs. They flooded the BIA office of visual aids and publications at the Haskell Institute in Lawrence, Kansas with requests for information and material. Religious publications of many types depicted with increasing frequency scenes of infant mortality, disease, and economic hopelessness on the reservations.[8]

Various church leaders soon became increasingly influential critics of BIA policy, the most effective of whom was Harold Fey of the *Christian Century*. The outspoken editor argued in favor of new programs based on concepts of humane Christianity and cultural pluralism. He recognized the inevitability of change, but maintained that recent actions destroyed essential Indian community life. Also, respect for different social structures in the process of developing reservation areas would foster the growth of a positive value system as well as a sense of personal security, identity, and worth.[9]

At about the same time the escalating fear of inheriting the many burdens left in the wake of federal withdrawal convinced some states to increase their resistance to administration policies. Senator William Langer of North Dakota, representing a northern plains state with some of the most severe Indian problems, led a fight to force the BIA to increase, rather than to reduce, its service responsibilities. Appearing before an appropriations subcommittee in 1955, he described a situation of virtual lawlessness on all three of his state's reservations and urged legislators to improve the grossly underfunded bureau law enforcement facilities.[10]

Langer also brought North Dakota state officials with him who testified that in an attempt to incorporate Indian recipients into state systems, the recent BIA reductions in funding levels for welfare unjustly dumped financial costs onto states with large Native American populations. State welfare boards had to serve Indians in cases qualifying for Social Security benefits or they would lose the matching fund subsidies for the entire state. But officials claimed that their lack of legal jurisdiction over reservations resulted in overpayment in some categories, such as Aid to Dependent Children, where regulations normally required attempts to determine parentage and to force a father to contribute before any welfare request would be granted. Although the state could take over legal and law enforcement systems under Public Law 280, it refused to do so without federal reimbursement of the costs.[11]

The remaining types of general assistance welfare were administered by county boards, and the BIA reimbursed them for Indian clients. The executive director of the North Dakota State Welfare Board related one example at the appropriation hearing of a near disaster because of diminishing bureau subsidies when the allocation for the Fort Berthold Reservation in 1954 ran out before the end of the year. The state legislature had always refused to contribute to general assistance for its Indian citizens. The bureau sent letters to doctors and hospitals serving Indian welfare cases, telling them to tighten eligibility and cut services "to the bone." Only a mild winter averted widespread and severe suffering.[12]

Since staunch proponents of termination and federal withdrawal dominated the BIA and the Indian affairs subcommittees, Senator Langer had to circumvent established policy-making channels to fight for change. He gained a forum to launch attacks on BIA policy when Estes Kefauver, chairman of the special Subcommittee to Investigate Juvenile Delinquency of the Senate Committee on the Judiciary on which Langer served, announced a series of hearings around the country on the causes of juvenile delinquency. The North Dakota Republican convinced him to include Indian reservations on the subcommittee's itinerary.[13]

Opponents of bureau policies appeared in force at the subsequent hearings in the fall of 1954 and again in the spring of 1955. Native Americans, various congressmen, and interested organizations described numerous desperate problems on reservations and agreed that only increased funding would improve conditions. Senator Langer contrasted the money spent on reservations—less than $100 million—with the billions sent overseas in foreign aid. The comparison of United States assistance to undeveloped countries with that to American Indians thereafter became a common tactic among the opposition.[14]

State officials testified at the juvenile delinquency hearings that the BIA did not give school districts enough money to incorporate Native American children into their systems. The bureau operated under the assumption that Indian education should be a state responsibility, and its complicated formula for dispensing aid attempted to pay local districts only for the difference between their income and the minimum sum deemed necessary to serve all the children in the area. Instead, state officials demanded per-capita payments to reimburse all additional costs and thus to equalize the financial burdens p!aced on various districts.[15]

Many witnesses at the hearings described how BIA policy had always discouraged Native Americans from developing their own resources. Lack of capital and the inability of Indians to obtain credit presented the biggest obstacles. Private lending institutions as well as the various government agencies, such as the Farm Home Administration, would usually not loan money to Indians because their trust property could not be used as collateral, and they rarely owned any other suitable assets. Emmons had recently altered BIA policy to permit trust lands to serve as loan security, but he had to reverse himself after legal questions raised by insurance companies led to a determination by the Department of Interior's solicitor that foreclosure would represent an unlawful termination of trust status.[16]

Indian farmers and ranchers told of various government projects that had left them deeply in debt. The cattle loan program of the 1930s had allotted too few head per Indian on small plots of land, and many operators subsequently failed because their ranches were not self-sustaining. The Revolving Fund Credit (RFC) program, enacted at the same time as part of the Indian Reorganization Act (IRA), gave too little, too late. The interest rates were good, but the loans were too small and restrictive. Many enterprises failed as a result, and Indians were blamed and labeled incompetent and lazy. When the BIA began phasing it out of existence, most Native Americans were left with no source of credit.[17]

The judiciary subcommittee concluded from the hearings that Indian juvenile delinquency resulted from poverty, neglect, and a life between two cultures. It suggested an aid program to help alleviate the problems and stressed the need to stimulate economic activity on reservations in a way that would bring about development without dislocating Indian communities and cultures. The subsequent committee report contrasted the distressed conditions on most reservations with an example of what could be done. In 1950 the Confederated Bands of Ute Indians in Utah had won a Claims Commission judgment against the United States government for $7.2 million. This money, together with funds coming in from leases on recently discovered oil and uranium fields, was divided among the northern, southern, and mountain Ute bands and used in a massive rehabilitation effort. The once poor and primitive Indians received, among other things, new homes, furniture, educational facilities, water systems, and livestock. But since only a few tribes could afford such projects, the judiciary subcommittee called for greatly increased federal funding and met with Emmons in early 1955 to discuss the matter.[18]

As pressure for more government financing of reservation development intensified, Emmons cautiously expanded his own program, still hoping that he could head off significant federal intervention by working with private businessmen. The first step in any effort was to perform resource surveys to determine a reservation's economic potential. The organization that the commissioner had put together in early 1954 to solicit grants from large foundations for such studies incorporated later that year as the American Indian Research Fund (AIRF), but it made little progress. When AIRF directors held a dinner in the spring of 1955 and invited foundation representatives, few attended and no one promised money. The group still lacked the funds even to hire a leader to actively pursue its goals.[19]

Thus, the only surveys completed at this time were financed by a few tribes who could afford to employ engineers on their own. The San Carlos and Jicarilla Apache tribal councils hired the Stanford Research Institute, an organization consisting of Stanford University instructors and centered in Palo Alto, California, to study their reservations. In addition to investigating resources, the researchers also attempted to apply American business techniques to Indian problems and recommended far-reaching changes in the tribes' political and economic structure to foster a spirit of competition and individual initiative.[20]

By the summer of 1955 Emmons's program for reservation development was clearly in trouble, and, to give it a boost, he brought the BIA more directly into the effort. He selected his assistant, Carl Beck, to head a project in which the bureau would act as liaison, arranging negotiations between tribes, industrialists, and local community officials to induce businessmen to locate factories on or near reservations. Emmons and Beck then launched a campaign to enlist cooperation and support for the program. In late 1955 they discussed the idea with a group of industrialists in Los Angeles and shortly thereafter approached the National Association of Manufacturers.[21]

When trying to convince audiences, Emmons and Beck emphasized the goal of freeing Indians from government dependence by providing them with a wage income and allowing them to compete individually with other Americans. They also stressed the skills that Indians allegedly possessed in working with their hands and the advantages of opening new sources of labor and developing new sales markets. Although never stated as such and often denied, the implication was that reservations were areas of cheap labor and that Native Americans could become consumers of manufactured goods.[22]

Under the new program, the BIA especially sought labor-intensive industries such as electronics, textiles, woodworking, and metal fabrication that could make use of the inexpensive work force yet not be severely handicapped by the lack of cheap transportation on isolated western reservations. Since Emmons's only goal was to obtain factory jobs for Native Americans, the arrangements that he tried to promote would leave businessmen in control of a reservation's economic development. The commissioner also knew that his program would compete with local and state governments and he therefore advised tribes that firms would expect lucrative incentives to locate near them. In many cases tribes were encouraged to provide inducements such as rent-free buildings or land on which to locate.[23]

In 1955, for example, Carl Beck reported to tribal representatives on the Sisseton Reservation in North Dakota that he knew of an electronics manufacturer who would furnish the raw materials and market the finished product in a joint venture. A firm in the nearby town of Sisseton, South Dakota wanted to expand its operations and had a building that could be used if someone would invest two or three thousand dollars for lights and work benches. Beck suggested that the tribe contribute that sum, but in this case the plans never developed.[24]

Naturally, those groups with a source of income were in a better position to attract industry, and the BIA encouraged them to use their money for that purpose. The Navajos received a steady flow of funds from oil and gas leases on their lands and worked out a program before most others. In December 1955 the Tribal Council appropriated $300,000 for plant construction and job training. Early the next year it employed an industrial manager, set up an industrialization department within its tribal administration, and began collaborating with local government and chambers of commerce in neighboring communities to bring private companies into the areas. The bureau also convinced the Fort Berthold Tribal Council to earmark $50,000 for industrial development out of money recently received from the government in return for the land taken to construct flood control projects on the Missouri River.[25]

Emmons proudly claimed that the BIA did not subsidize private businesses under his program. The money came either from tribal funds or out of the pockets of Indian workers; if a tribe had no income the commissioner suggested that it borrow the money and then repay it through a payroll deduction after a company began operating. The only benefit to Native Americans would be the creation of new jobs, but even that was usually not certain. Emmons encouraged the requirement of a certain percentage of Indian workers in factories under negotiated contracts, but firms were reluctant to accept restrictions on their labor force, and therefore most agreements did not include such provisions.[26]

Another program, adult education, was initiated at this time at least partly to counter the intensifying opposition to the policy of withdrawal and to dramatize Emmons's "three-prong attack" on reservation problems. One BIA official in the education branch did not see the program as a wise use of tight dollars since it was not based on concrete information to determine the need or projected benefits; he related an episode that allegedly was the impetus for starting the project, although he stressed that the story came to him indirectly, and he therefore could not verify it. While on a trip to Florida, Emmons asked a group of traditional Seminoles if they would like to learn to speak English, but the interpreter translated the question as "the Commissioner would like you to raise your hands." Naturally most of the Indians responded. Emmons was impressed and described the incident on numerous occasions to show the enthusiasm toward his adult education program. Whatever the case, the project was launched in 1955 on five reservations: Papago in Arizona, Fort Hall in Idaho, Rosebud in South Dakota, Turtle Mountain in North Dakota, and Seminole in Florida. It was expanded thereafter until it reached over sixty locations before the end of Emmons's term. The goal was to contribute to the general emphasis on Indian assimilation by teaching adults without an education enough fundamental reading, speaking, and computing skills to operate in the non-Indian world.[27]

Meanwhile, various congressmen followed the path forged by Senator Langer's juvenile delinquency hearings and launched new attacks on BIA policy. They initiated moves to alter it and tried to obtain more federal money from the bureau to ease the burden on their respective states. Following the hearings, the Senate appropriations subcommittee that handled Department of the Interior funding demanded a bureau report to determine what more was needed to meet federal responsibilities toward Indian education. In early 1956 Oklahoma senators Robert Kerr and A. S. Mike Monroney requested higher educational subsidies for states before the appropriations subcommittee. Representative John Rhodes and Senator Barry Goldwater of Arizona then introduced resolutions into both houses of Congress calling for a national study to help find solutions to the serious deficiencies in Indian education. The proposals were quickly amended to include an investigation of the funding problem. Although Congress ultimately passed such a measure and granted higher subsidies to states, it never financed the study of Indian education.[28]

Other congressional opponents of BIA policy tried to expand federal efforts to improve economic opportunity in Indian areas. Senators Langer and Kefauver brought out a measure that would direct the secretary of commerce to conduct resource surveys on Indian lands, thereby circumventing the reluctant Department of the Interior. Senators James Murray and Mike Mansfield and Representative Lee Metcalf of Montana went even further and tied reservation development into a legislative package that congressional liberals were formulating to stimulate the recently recessed national economy. They wrote to Illinois Senator Paul Douglas in early 1956 and convinced him to include reservations in a proposal he had introduced that would give federal loans and grants to depressed areas for industrialization. Neither measure made significant progress at this time, but more would follow.[29]

Relocation, a program created largely to eliminate the need for expensive reservation development, also came increasingly under attack. Senator Murray and Representative Metcalf urged Emmons to grant more assistance to Indians who moved to cities, while Senator Mansfield questioned the underlying motives of relocation, noting that Native Americans lost their eligibility for federal aid once they had left the reservation.[30]

Two articles in March 1956 in liberal magazines widely read by both Indians and non-Indians proved especially damaging to the BIA. Ruth Mulvey Harmer's "Uprooting the Indians" in *Atlantic Monthly* told of extremely bleak conditions confronting relocatees in the move as well as upon arrival in cities. "The Raid on the Reservations" by Dorothy Van De Mark in *Harper's Magazine* described relocation as a policy motivated by the drive to remove Indians from their land so non-Indians could get it. A stormy debate followed. The Letters to the Editor sections in subsequent issues of both magazines contained rebuttals to the articles by Emmons, Assistant Indian Commissioner Barton Greenwood, and Assistant Secretary of the Interior Wesley D'Ewart. Historian Angie Debo, Laverne Madigan of the AAIA, and the authors defended the pieces.[31]

Emmons met the criticism from inside and outside of Congress with an increase in relocation aid and an acceleration of his own efforts to deal with reservation problems without costly rehabilitation projects. He altered the bureau structure to reflect a new emphasis on economic development by uplifting several of its offices and creating a new Division of Tribal Programs and Relocation under an assistant commissioner. Moreover, Congress agreed to á BIA request to more than triple the funding for relocation in 1956. The bureau opened additional relocation offices in St. Louis, San Francisco, and San Jose and made small grants available for essential household goods, furniture, or clothing "to bring [an Indian's] appearance up to acceptable standards." The BIA also agreed to pay for vocational training and basic education as well as medical insurance for one year.[32]

In the summer of 1956 Representative Ed Edmondson of Oklahoma, E. Y. Berry of South Dakota, and Stewart Udall of Arizona introduced a measure that would subsidize Indian trade or vocational education for up to two years. They intended it to work in conjunction with both the relocation program and the BIA effort to attract industry to reservations. The proposal enjoyed widespread support. Most Native Americans and bureau opponents welcomed any economic aid to Indians, while terminationists thought of it as an attempt to remove the so-called surplus population from reservations. Since Congress had recently been granting sizable appropriations to similar programs for other groups, proponents successfully promoted the bill as an extension of American citizenship rights, rather than a special service. It became Public Law 959 in August.[33]

Most of the money under the bill would pay tuition and expenses for Native Americans enrolled in trade schools in cities where they relocated. The rest would go directly to companies that had contracted to locate factories near reservations under the BIA's industrialization program. After the approval of cooperating firms as training facilities, the bureau would reimburse businesses for 50 percent of the legal minimum wage for each Indian in return for on-the-job training. Often, the BIA even screened and enlisted potential workers and thus lowered recruitment costs.[34]

Emmons also initiated action in response to recent criticism after the joint termination hearings to suggest greater Indian participation in the creation of policy affecting them. In late 1955 Homer Jenkins, the bureau's director of program planning, had announced before the annual meeting of the Governors' Interstate Indian Council that the agency was formulating a new approach to "emancipating" Native Americans under which Indians would become partners in planning, rather than reluctant recipients of programs. Then on April 12, 1956, Emmons issued an important memorandum which called for BIA officials to work with Native Americans in drawing up their own course of action for social and economic development. They were to help Indians decide on methods of reaching a state of self-reliance and to find alternate ways of financing programs because of the limited availability of federal funds. But since tribes rarely had money or expertise to begin projects on their own, they could participate only within established bureau goals and policies.[35]

From July until December 1956, the commissioner held a series of meetings with tribal representatives to encourage them to take part in planning under the April 12 memo and to show evidence of consultation in response to recent criticism of neglecting Indian opinion. Emmons also wanted to promote his own brand of development programs over those gaining an increased following among his opponents. BIA officials conducted conferences covering specific bureau area divisions in various western cities and invited the top three tribal representatives from every group within the region to participate. Emmons met briefly with individual tribal delegations, and each session included general assemblies of all the groups. The commissioner also took precautions to ensure that "there would be no outside interruptions." He chose locations far removed from the native habitats of the groups at a particular session. In addition, uninvited Indians and members of the press were not allowed to attend.[36]

Throughout the conferences many tribal leaders took advantage of the opportunity to voice grievances over bureau policies. Some saw education as an avenue of escape from reservation poverty and demanded more facilities. Hopi Tribal Chairman Karl Johnson said that his people were "a bit jealous" over the efforts on the Navajo Reservation and wanted to know why the BIA did not undertake similar programs elsewhere. Emmons replied that he attacked the biggest problem first, but other delegates described conditions similar to those among the Navajos on many reservations. Tribal Secretary James Monteau of Montana's Rocky Boy Reservation, for example, reported that two of that group's three schools had been condemned for over ten years and the third for over six years. When several Indians called on Emmons to provide more money for college education, he agreed that Congress had not been generous with scholarship money and that the $70,000 appropriated that year was only a "drop in the bucket."[37]

Many delegates complained that particular BIA educational policies would destroy their cultures, break up their families, and hinder their children's learning and self-image. Hopi leaders noted that many teachers at bureau schools were prejudiced against Indians and insisted that the tribe should have a greater role in evaluating personnel. Numerous other tribal representatives protested recent efforts to integrate their children into public schools. Some maintained that high rates of absenteeism and early drop-outs stemmed from feelings of embarrassment and inferiority when students with tattered clothes from poor families were forced to mix with wealthier non-Indians and encounter cruel peer group treatment.[38]

Others objected to transferring their children to public schools many miles away from homes and families. Navajo parents lamented that the acculturation that resulted from such a process eroded traditional authority, values, and community life and left everyone in a state of confusion. Havasupai families in Arizona had even risked trouble with the United States Park Service by moving into the Grand Canyon National Park so their children could attend schools in the nearby town of Grand Canyon rather than the distant boarding schools of the BIA.[39]

Several Indians expressed a fear of arbitrary state takeover of law-and-order jurisdiction on their reservations under the authority of Public Law 280. This 1953 legislation allowed states outside of the five specified for immediate assumption of responsibilities to acquire jurisdiction by act of their legislature or constitutional amendment. Native Americans knew little about state systems and anticipated discrimination under them. But they had little to worry about at this time since few states were willing to assume law-and-order responsibilities without federal repayment of the additional expenses and since most were aware of the unpopularity of such a move among their native citizens. In 1955 the Nevada legislature had passed such a measure, but it allowed any county to be exempted from the law if it chose. In practice, state officials consulted tribes first anyway. Two years later South Dakota and Washington enacted takeover bills, but the Washington law provided for prior consent, and the South Dakota measure was never implemented because it was contingent upon federal reimbursement that was never forthcoming.[40]

Serious problems, however, sometimes developed on reservations in the five states that acquired jurisdiction over Indian lands immediately following enactment of Public Law 280. At the Aberdeen Area Conference Omaha Tribal Chairman Gustavus White described the desperate situation on his Nebraska reservation after the BIA removed its facilities and law enforcement personnel from the state. Because Thurston County lacked the money and the willingness to extend services over the reservation, a virtual state of lawlessness promptly resulted.[41]

Although some Native Americans approved of the relocation program as an opportunity for individual economic advancement, it came under increasing attack after the critical treatments in recent magazine articles. To the tribal leaders who questioned the motives of the program at the various area conferences, Emmons responded, "There are some people, as you know, that want to keep the Indian as a museum piece. They believe that Indians ought to be kept on the reservation in spite of the fact that they can't make a living there." The commissioner frequently brought one of the articles into conversations, commenting at one point that "it sort of makes me sick at heart and disgusted when some woman writer will write an article like there was in *Harper's Magazine* . . . trying to create suspicion in the minds of the Indian people themselves." Each time he told his audiences that the author of "The Raid on the Reservations" had changed her point of view and supported his policies after he had discussed the issues at length with her.[42]

Some tribal representatives also protested the BIA's recruitment tactics, its treatment of relocating Indians, and the living conditions in cities participating in the relocation program. Blackfoot Tribal Secretary Iliff McKay reported that the bureau was refusing requests for welfare aid and instead was encouraging people to relocate. Pine Ridge Tribal Secretary Charles Little Hawk told of stories coming from relocatees in California that Indians were forced to live in the area's dirtiest slums.[43]

Most of the attacks at the conference were directed at the impact of the population movement on tribes. Paul Bernal, the tribal secretary of Taos Pueblo, complained about how relocation disrupted patterns of religious and community responsibilities. Tribal members, for example, had to perform services such as cleaning ditches to earn the use of irrigation water for their land, but after moving to cities, people did not do the community work nor take care of their property. Numerous delegates pointed out that the program eliminated the most likely candidates for tribal leadership by removing the youngest and most skilled members. This left an unbalanced population of those least able to make the tribe economically viable and thus encouraged further attempts to liquidate reservations.[44]

Many tribal representatives at the conferences concluded that the money appropriated for relocation could be better spent on rehabilitating reservations so Indians could make a living in their homelands. Omaha Tribal Chairman Gustavus White pointed to the government factories that had employed Native Americans in the construction of aircraft during World War II and asked "why can't the government do this in peace time the same as in war?" Some delegates protested bureau land policies. They called instead for help in financing a series of purchases and exchanges to reduce the problem of non-Indian land intermingled with Indian property and thus allow the consolidation of tribal holdings so they could be used for various group enterprises. Others pleaded for a loosening of credit policies so they could develop their own resources. The Yavapai Apaches, for example, wanted loans that would allow them to buy farm equipment to work their own land rather than having to lease it to outsiders.[45]

Emmons insisted that Congress would not finance any such schemes and attempted to convince the Indians to accept relocation and try to attract industry to reservation areas. When an exasperated BIA agency superintendent complained that Indians would rather starve on their homelands than move to cities, Emmons suggested that it was a matter of educating them into relocating so the remaining residents could make a living after the "surplus population" was reduced.[46]

Emmons and BIA officials frequently denied that these conferences were a disguised effort to achieve terminationist goals and maintained that they were a protective move. They told Indians that if Congress detected no progress under the bureau it would pass a drastic measure such as the bill introduced nearly every session by Nevada Senator George Malone to abolish the BIA within three years. But the way that the bureau concluded each conference clearly revealed a goal of showing grassroots support for an increasingly controversial policy.[47]

Blackfoot Tribal Secretary Iliff McKay later related how the BIA gained Indian endorsement at the conference in Salt Lake City. Tribal representatives were instructed to prepare resolutions for adoption by the assembly. Bureau personnel handed out samples from previous sessions that expressed unqualified support for Emmons's programs and applauded his stand against ending reservation life and his promotion of the general welfare. Officials suggested that the Indians might like to draw up similar ones, but they wrote their own versions and eliminated most of the praise.[48]

On the final day of the Salt Lake City conference, Emmons received copies of the resolutions, which he pronounced unacceptable unless certain amendments were made. The assembly complied, and the commissioner then told the delegates in a formal address how gratifying it was that they approved of his programs and that he could now go before Congress with evidence of real Indian support. Nevertheless, at many of the conferences, tribal leaders still passed critical resolutions, ranging from demands for Indian consent before the construction of federal projects on reservations to threats of noncompliance in the implementation of the April 12 memo. A few months later the NCAI at its annual convention denounced the BIA's method of choosing and limiting tribal delegations and accused Emmons of misrepresenting. Indian views.[49]

But the conferences' impact on public relations seemed to be a success according to bureau goals. A Washington, D.C. newspaper published a muckraking piece on the conferences, but most others reported that Native Americans praised BIA policies. Earl Pomeroy wrote an article in the *Denver Post* headlined "Indians Endorse Plans to End Underdog Role." The *Portland Oregonian* told readers that "support for the commissioner's program has been virtually unanimous among the tribes he has met with in the West." It went on to say that "proof of this support was shown by Emmons when he passed out resolutions from the Indians, all praising, commending, and endorsing the Commissioner's program."[50]

While Emmons was conducting the conferences, the BIA was furthering its efforts to withdraw from Indian affairs. Although after all of the negative press coverage he preferred to call it "readjustment," Emmons still promoted termination and used the bureau's influence to try to achieve it. In the summer of 1956 the Indian affairs subcommittees considered a proposal that would restore the ownership of 818,000 acres to the Confederated Tribes of the Colville Reservation in Washington. The land was classified as surplus; that is, it remained undisposed after the reservation had been divided into allotments under the 1887 Dawes Severalty Act. BIA officials at the Portland area office tried to get the Colvilles to agree to a termination plan before the bureau would recommend that the subcommittees report out a bill for the land-title transfer. When the Indians proved reluctant, the subcommittees amended the measure at the BIA's insistence to require the tribe's business council to submit within five years a plan for the removal of federal supervision and trust status. The proposal passed in this form, and the Indians received the land, but Congress never terminated the group.[51]

The sentiment for termination had already faded considerably by 1956, and the only bills passed that year involved tribes that closely resembled those successfully acted upon two years earlier. The president signed measures covering the Wyandotte, Peoria, and Ottawa groups of Oklahoma, all of which were small and comparatively assimilated. Moreover, they owned little property and lacked the unity to even make much of an attempt at tribal government.[52]

The bureau claimed that the three Oklahoma bands were agreeable to termination, but in at least one case, tribal officials later pointed to intense BIA pressure. Ottawa council member Walter Gene Jennison said that the bureau urged cooperation and a council vote of approval since Congress would terminate the tribe no matter how it acted. In addition, the BIA held out incentive in the form of a promise of free college education for the young. The tribe apparently assumed that this would last forever and was thus surprised when it was discontinued after five years. Another Ottawa, Charles E. Dawes, reported that the bureau convinced the group that its case before the Indians Claims Commission for over $143 million would get processed much more quickly if it went along with termination.[53]

The BIA also accelerated efforts to transfer some of its service activities, including a new emphasis on tribal assumption of various functions in line with the April 12 memo which had called for greater Indian participation in withdrawal planning. Most of the attempts at this point involved the management of reservation resources. On non-grazing lands, for example, the bureau proposed to eliminate its soil-and-range-conservation operations by integrating Indian holdings into the Bureau of Land Management's soil conservation districts. It achieved limited success in this area, either by organizing reservations into new districts or by incorporating them into established ones. In 1956 the Big Sandy Soil Conservation District in Arizona agreed to serve the Hualapai and Fort Mohave reservations, and Indians on the Colorado River Reservation formed the Parker Valley Soil Conservation District.[54]

On grazing lands the BIA had traditionally funded range-improvement projects and the enforcement of grazing regulations, but tribal councils had recently begun appropriating their own money at the bureau's urging to assume the responsibility themselves. In some cases, however, councils failed to enforce regulations or to fund conservation programs adequately because Indian cattlemen dominated tribal governments and were reluctant to tax or exercise authority over colleagues. Thus, the BIA sometimes pressured councils into passing range ordinances and fees.[55]

The Hualapais in Arizona, for example, had recently been paying the bureau for its operation of a well-pumping plant and a system of hauling water to cattle. In 1957 the tribe could no longer afford to continue the arrangements and asked the BIA for help, but before it gave the Hualapais any money, the bureau required them to adopt grazing fees and regulations. Only the Papago, San Carlos, and Fort Apache tribal councils passed additional ordinances before the end of Emmons's term in office. As pressure for termination subsided, the BIA no longer anticipated immediate withdrawal and shifted its emphasis to educational programs to encourage Indians to gradually take over soil-and-range-conservation operations.[56]

The bureau also attempted at the same time to integrate Native Americans into the various resource management positions on reservations to replace BIA personnel as they withdrew. The branch of forestry at the Mescalero agency initiated a training program to prepare Indians to assume certain forest responsibilities. At first officials emphasized areas like fire protection, which required the least instruction, and later turned to more advanced skills such as appraising timber, contracting, advertising, sales, and pricing. Similar efforts resulted in more Indian members on the Navajo forestry and fire-control staff and among the ranks of forester aids on the Fort Apache Reservation. But the bureau could not train Native Americans fast enough, and non-Indians continued to hold most higher-level jobs.[57]

# 7

# Growing Battle
# over Development

In the 1956 elections Democrats enlarged their congressional majority over the slight leads of two years earlier. The Republicans lost the chairmanship of the Senate Committee on Interior and Insular Affairs in the reshuffling of assignments, and liberal James E. Murray of Montana replaced the conservative George Malone of Nevada who had introduced bills to abolish the BIA every session since the early 1950s. Democrats appointed liberal Richard Neuberger of Oregon to head the Senate Indian Affairs Subcommittee. The result was less agreement between branches of government in the formation of Indian policy and, most important, a mounting battle over how reservations should be rehabilitated and developed economically.

This issue vividly reflected the fundamental ideological differences between the opposing forces. Conservative terminationists believed that modern corporate capitalism, or the process of industrial development under the leadership of private businessmen, represented the best and most advanced of developmental schemes. They operated under the notion that this was a natural, self-regulating mechanism that would function well for everyone if not interfered with by outside forces such as government regulation or a competing system like an anachronistic communal tribalism. Therefore, their view of America was somewhat monolithic, and they believed that assimilation into the dominant social and economic structure should be a universal goal. Although they frequently maintained that their policies were not intended to destroy Indian cultures, they accepted a very narrow definition of culture that did not go much beyond arts, crafts, and memories of a heritage.

Critics of termination and federal withdrawal, however, had less faith in the total beneficence of unfettered corporate capitalism. Although most were certainly capitalists in general, they did not necessarily see that system as the epitome of social and economic structures. They placed less emphasis on adherence to a particular cultural or economic mode and were more willing to allow Native Americans to exist in a separate realm within a diverse America. This was somewhat reminiscent of the view of cultural pluralism, or cultural relativity, accepted by the 1920s and 1930s generation of reformers led by John Collier, which saw social and economic structures developing as responses to particular environments rather than moving historically in a progressive, straightforward fashion, with each representing an advance over the other. And since these reformers did not fear government involvement and spending as much as conservatives, they were not as reluctant to use federal dollars to aid in development programs that would operate within the context of Indian cultures and with a significant degree of independent sovereignty.

By about early 1957 opposition to Emmons's policies intensified as controversial Native American issues increasingly attracted the attention of journalists, who were even more widely read than most previous critics. Carl Rowan, for example, wrote a fifteen-part series for the *Minneapolis Tribune*, entitled "The First Are Last," on conditions in the increasing numbers of Indian slums, such as Minneapolis's "City of Hope" district. Moreover, he described the plight of Native Americans in terms similar to those of the emerging black civil rights movement, writing of racism and racial sterotypes. Popular columnist and commentator Paul Harvey followed shortly thereafter with a piece that accused the government of neglecting Indians in Arizona. He called for a national effort on reservations similar to the proposed "Point Four" program of distributing economic and technical aid to underdeveloped countries.[1]

The continuing publicity stimulated even more interest and demands for change. In mid-February the Montana legislature unanimously passed a memorial which urged the state's congressional delegation to support the principle of federal responsibility toward all Indians. Several weeks later the Fund for the Republic established a five-man Commission on the Rights and Reponsibilities of the American Indian to study policies affecting Native Americans. Former Indian commissioner William A. Brophy served as executive director. Other members included

Charles A. Sprague, publisher of the *Oregon Statesman* in Salem, Karl Llewellyn, Professor of Jurisprudence at the University of Chicago, Arthur M. Schlesinger, Sr., Professor Emeritus at Harvard University, and William W. Keeler, vice-president of Phillips Petroleum Company and chief of the Cherokee Nation.[2]

About the same time, the Council of the Episcopal Diocese of Chicago called for the modification of House Concurrent Resolution 108, a consent amendment to Public Law 280, changes in the relocation program, and the economic development of reservations. Reverend Dr. Vine Deloria, a Sioux and the assistant secretary in charge of Indian work in the Division of Domestic Missions of the Episcopal Church, suggested an effort similar to the "Point Four" plan and added that Native Americans needed to be shown how to modernize in ways within Indian traditions.[3]

Meanwhile, Emmons was trying to further his economic development program that would attract established industries to locate on or near reservations. With opponents increasingly demanding a greater federal commitment toward the industrialization effort, the commissioner wanted to set up pilot plants throughout the West to prove the feasibility of his own plans. But his hope that the American Indian Research Fund (AIRF), which he had organized earlier, could win the support of private foundations for the preliminary surveys of reservations was not being realized. Most rejections of AIRF requests were based upon charter prohibitions against anything that might affect legislative policy.[4]

Emmons concluded that he might have to turn to government financing of the reservation studies, but he wanted to ensure that the federal role would go no further. The commissioner hoped somehow to get a couple of surveys started which could serve as examples on other reservations to stimulate his program of attracting outside industries. When Agricultural Research Services (ARS), which had received a contract to get information for a congresssional proposal to deal with the recent national recession, asked the BIA if it had any areas to include in a preliminary investigation of the economic potential in certain depressed regions of the country, the bureau named the Papago Reservation in Arizona and Pine Ridge Reservation in South Dakota. Both of these groups remained among the poorest and least developed of all tribes and had heard promises and congressional proposals for their rehabilitation since the early 1950s. But since the ARS surveys never materialized, the Indians had to wait, and Emmons's program moved slowly.[5]

A few small companies entered into agreements with tribes and the BIA in 1956, but Native Americans benefited little. With tribes providing much of the "risk investment" in the form of various types of inducements, businessmen had little of their own interest at stake and thus found it easy simply to leave if the plan did not go well. Although the commissioner repeatedly emphasized that firms should be reputable and not "fly-by-night" outfits, the bureau frequently encouraged companies with questionable qualifications in its haste to achieve results. Not until 1964 did officials closely scrutinize industries and discourage financially unstable enterprises from participating.[6]

In May 1956 Saddlecraft, Incorporated of Knoxville, Tennessee set up a branch near the Cherokee Reservation in North Carolina and hired 21 Indian workers to turn out moccasins and other leather goods. The next month the production manager of Baby Line Furniture Company, who had employed many Native Americans for the firm's main plant in Los Angeles under the relocation program, negotiated a contract with the Navajo Tribal Council. In return for a suitable site and a $200,000 subsidy from the tribe, the company agreed to establish Navajo Furniture Industries in Gamerco, New Mexico and to give the Indians one-fourth of the profits from the manufacture of children's furniture, house shutters, and similar products. The BIA estimated that within a year the factory would employ 100 Navajos, but at the end of that period 10 were on the payroll and only 9 more were added before Emmons left office.[7]

A few months later Lear, Incorporated of Santa Monica, California opened the Lear-Navajo plant at Flagstaff, Arizona to assemble electrical components. The Navajos invested heavily in the venture, including $2250 payments for an appropriate building. The bureau again predicted that it would soon employ 100 Indians, but only 20 worked there when it closed the next year after succumbing to the economic recession.[8]

In early 1957 the BIA, which had just increased the supply of credit somewhat in response to criticism of its tight policies, began to allow tribes to use Revolving Fund loan money to attract industry. When combined with an even greater effort by the bureau and the availability of vocational training subsidies under the recently enacted Public Law 959, it helped bring more factories into the program that year, but the results proved little better than before. Early in the year Martin S. Meyers and Associates of Los Angeles established Zuni Industries on the Zuni Reservation in New Mexico and hired a few Indians to make ceramic products, such as mosaic table tops. White Tree's Workshop located on the Cherokee Reservation in North Carolina and employed a handful of Native Americans in the production of souvenirs. Tatanka Company came to McLaughlin, South Dakota and hired three Sioux Indians from the nearby Standing Rock Reservation to make toys. Sixteen Navajos found work constructing custom furniture at the new Kingman Industries in Kingman, Arizona, but the outfit folded within a year.[9]

The case of the Flandreau Garment Factory that same year especially revealed the governing philosophy of incorporating reservations into the existing industrial network under the leadership of non-Indian businessmen rather than encouraging tribal enterprises. A plant in Flandreau, South Dakota had operated since the 1930s under bureau management, selling its garments to BIA schools and hospitals in a closed market. The Emmons administration closed it in 1955 under its policy of cutting anything that competed with private industry. Thereafter, the bureau purchased garments on the open market from outside businesses and encouraged the unemployed Santee Sioux to relocate in eastern cities where similar textile operations could put their skills to use. The Indians naturally hated losing the factory and wanted a chance to run it themselves. But the BIA brought in outside businessmen who took advantage of the vocational training subsidy, reopened the plant, and began producing ladies' apparel.[10]

The bureau also continued to exaggerate grossly the projected employment figures in order to cast a positive image on its program. When Parsons and Baker Manufacturing Company of Phoenixville, Pennsylvania opened Casa Grande Mills in 1957 to make garments at Casa Grande, Arizona, officials boasted that it would use 125 Pima and Papago Indians immediately and eventually as many as 700. But after seventeen months of operation, the entire work force consisted of 74 whites and a Pima woman. In the case of New Moon Homes of Alma, Michigan, the bureau estimated that the firm would hire and train 100 Sioux to manufacture house trailers within a year after it opened a plant in Rapid City, South Dakota. But at the end of that time, only 12 were on the payroll. When Bayly Manufacturing Company of Yakima, Washington found the vocational training program appealing and expanded its garment factory, the BIA announced that 100 more Yakimas would be employed, but only 10 were actually added.[11]

An agreement with a firm that established First Americans, Incorporated, in Lame Deer, Montana in 1957 also revealed how much companies could gain under the program, even if tribes did not. The factory was started at virtually no risk to the owner. The site cost nothing since it was a former school building on tribal land, local citizens donated the machinery, the power company gave enough free electricity to get started, and a nearby sawmill supplied the scrap wood that provided much of the firm's raw material needs. Since the contract called for the production of fishing tackle which required a relatively intricate assembly process, the BIA allowed eight weeks of wage subsidies under the on-the-job training program rather than the three weeks normally · granted in less complex types of work. But once in operation, the company made simple necktie racks and pocketed the additional subsidies. As in the other cases, the bureau distorted the employment figures, announcing a projection of 125 positions within a year that in reality turned out to be about 24.[12]

Despite the lengthy list of new industries near reservations, progress remained insignificant compared to the total need. Even according to Emmons's inflated figures, only 500 more Indians had jobs than before. The BIA's program was not going well because of a number of serious problems in attracting companies. The stalled effort to perform surveys of reservations, for example, meant that corporate executives did not have access to information vital in making a decision to locate, such as the availability of natural resources, the quantity and quality of the work force, or access to transportation. In addition, some entrepreneurs were reluctant to make a commitment in negotiating with the BIA and tribes because trust arrangements on Indian lands made them apprehensive about government regulations.[13]

Other obstacles included the lack of facilities and services necessary for manufacturing, such as electrical power, water, housing, and communications. Transportation, however, presented the biggest problem because few roads or railroads existed near reservations. Even for those firms that could surmount that difficulty by producing items for the local market, the demand for such goods in sparsely populated and poverty-stricken regions of the West was limited. Furthermore, the available labor supply acted as a deterrent to many types of businesses since Native Americans were the least-educated minority group in the country, and their level of industrial skill measured far below the national average. A study by the comptroller general of the BIA's progress in withdrawal activities concluded that many problems stemmed from the chaotic lack of planning and absence of written criteria for conducting negotiations with prospective firms in the bureau program.[14]

The condition of the national economy made matters even worse. In 1957 the BIA opened new relocation offices in Dallas, Texas; Cincinnati and Cleveland, Ohio; and Joliet and Waukegan, Illinois, in an attempt to expand that program to step up its own solution to Indian problems in the face of increasing agitation for more costly projects. But the recent recession deepened and therefore dramatically slowed relocation when the bureau could no longer find enough jobs for Native Americans in urban areas. This slowdown, in turn, resulted in more pressure on reservation industrial development since it remained the only alternative policy for improving the economic status of Indians. But the recession made businessmen reluctant to expand operations anywhere in the nation. Moreover, the labor-intensive types of manufacturing which had found Indian labor an attractive incentive to enter into the bureau's program began to experience serious competition from foreign countries such as Japan.[15]

The worsening recession and the languishing BIA program encouraged congressional opponents of bureau policy to intensify their drive to extend vastly the government role in stimulating reservation economies. The catalyst for further action came when the Defense Department announced its intention to close the Turtle Mountain Ordnance Plant at Rolla, North Dakota in early 1957. This branch of the Bulova Watch Company had manufactured jewel bearings under contract for the past four and one-half years. Although the Rolla factory was started before the recent interest in industrial development, many viewed it as a prototype and symbol of the possibilities of an enlarged federal program.[16]

North Dakota Senator William Langer called a meeting to discuss the matter on January 7, 1957, and legislators from eleven western states attended. They all agreed to exert pressure to keep the ordnance factory open, but ironically the most persuasive argument was national defense. Some contended that closing the military's only source of jewel bearings would result in a dependence on a foreign supplier, who might be easily cut off in wartime. Even more important, the conference resulted in a proposed bill, S. 809, sponsored by Langer and cosponsored by twenty other senators. The measure called for $20 million in loans and grants to Native Americans for establishing tribal enterprises or individual Indian businesses or for loans to non-Indian companies which fulfilled the purposes of the act.[17]

When S. 809 reached the Senate Indian Affairs Subcommittee, the new chairman, Democrat Richard Neuberger of Oregon, took advantage of the opportunity to assail the Eisenhower administration's entire Indian policy. He scheduled hearings on the measure for the end of March 1957, and at the same time added two more bills for consideration that had been introduced in previous congressional sessions but had received no attention from the subcommittee. Senate Concurrent Resolution 3 declared a United States policy of bringing Native American communities up to the material standards of non-Indian areas and thus essentially repudiated House Concurrent Resolution 108. Bill S. 331 would amend Public Law 280 to provide for Indian consent before any state takeover of law-and-order jurisdiction on reservations.[18]

Numerous Native Americans appeared at the hearings to testify in favor of all three proposals. Speaking for the Department of the Interior, Acting Secretary Hatfield Chilson opposed Senate Concurrent Resolution 3 because it implied that the BIA had not been providing the kinds of services the measure called for and because it would raise Indian expectations beyond the government's willingness to pay. Furthermore, he contended that the bureau's program was sufficient and that most reservations would still not be able to support their populations.[19]

When Emmons appeared to defend his policies, Neuberger questioned him aggressively, drawing him into the sharpest debate yet over the fundamental wisdom and soundness of the whole withdrawal and termination policy. Speaking of the many Native Americans who had testified in favor of the proposals that would reject the controversial new direction in Indian affairs, the sena-

tor noted that they "feel very sincerely that the termination policy has been used as a justification for abandoning many of the
services to the Indians." He suggested that the bill terminating
the Klamaths in his home state was motivated by the desire for
Indian land by referring to the "hasty liquidation" and "fire-sale
distribution" of Klamath assets that was already in progress.
The commissioner agreed that the bill needed amendments but
defended termination as a general policy that would convince Indians that they would not remain under the paternalism of Washington. He saw it as the fulfillment of a long-standing national
goal that Native Americans be "integrated in the regular American
population" and also as a matter of maturing into that improved
and more advanced state: "I think on the whole the Indians of
this country will someday reach the age of twenty-one. It is
probably high time that the Indians begin to plan toward that
eventuality."[20]

Many critics of the BIA immediately endorsed S. 809. At the
annual Association on American Indian Affairs (AAIA) convention, Oliver La Farge attacked the bureau's program because it resulted in Indians working in factories owned by outsiders and
urged the administration to support Langer's proposal so more
could find work in Native American enterprises. Emmons took
the offensive in response to recent attacks and to the growing
strength of the congressional opposition. He granted a press interview in April 1957 in which he stressed "the brighter side of
the Indian picture," describing progress under the relocation program and his accomplishments in attracting industry to reservations. In trying to appear as successful as possible, however, the
commissioner quoted the wildly optimistic employment projec-
tions that had already proven very inaccurate. At this time, S.
809 failed, but the fight over how to develop Indian areas economically was far from over.[21]

Meanwhile, resurgent opponents of BIA withdrawal from Indian affairs continued to push for a greater federal effort in the
attack on reservation problems. Even after the transfer of health
responsibilities to the Public Health Service (PHS) in 1955, the
Department of the Interior still controlled expenditures for new
hospitals. But it refused to authorize the construction of new projects because it wanted to keep its budget down and to integrate
Native Americans into existing facilities that catered to other

citizens. As a result, money appropriated for construction accumulated in the treasury until fiscally conservative congressmen noticed the unspent surplus and tried to cut funding for Indian health. At the same time, serious shortages existed in some areas with high concentrations of Native American population because communities lacked the financial base to construct hospitals that the bureau could contract with for the care of Indian patients.[22]

To eliminate what they saw as delay tactics by an agency trying to work its way out of existence and to bring health services to more reservations, members of the Montana delegation introduced measures in both houses of Congress that would allow the United States surgeon general to give grants to communities to assist in the construction of hospitals that would serve both Indians and non-Indians or to build federal facilities without going through the Department of the Interior if he felt it was necessary. The Department of Health, Education, and Welfare approved of the proposal, seeing it as another tool in its new and very difficult task of bringing better care to Indians through the PHS. But the Department of the Interior thought that aid under the bill was too open-ended and preferred a more restrictive plan. The measure became law in August 1957, owing in large part to the fact that proponents bypassed the unreceptive House Indian Affairs Subcommittee in favor of the Subcommittee on Health and Science of the Committee on Interstate and Foreign Commerce.[23]

The escalating debate over how to develop reservations also gave new life to recent criticism of BIA policy toward Indian land. Opponents charged that in trying to cut the acreage in trust status, the bureau encouraged sales to non-Indians and actually contributed to the decline of reservation economies by reducing the land base on which tribal enterprise depended. When, in an attempt to counter the increasingly bad press on the issue, the BIA issued a press release in early summer of 1957 entitled "Over 1,000,000 Acres Added to Indian Tribal Land Holdings in Last Three Years," Representative Lee Metcalf accused the agency of outright deceit. He claimed that the bureau's figures were misleading because sales to non-Indians during the same period had really resulted in a net loss of acreage. The Montana Democrat also pointed out that over three-fourths of the total in the BIA statistics consisted of the unsold "surplus" lands deeded back to the Colvilles and thus could not be considered a gain since the tribe had never sanctioned the cession in the first place.[24]

At the same time, Senator Richard Neuberger led his Indian Affairs Subcommittee into an investigation of the impact of the notorious policy change of May 16, 1955, which had declared that approval for granting title changes on trust allotments would no longer be denied because of possible injury to a tribal timber or grazing unit. He concluded that the action endangered conservation practices as well as reservation economies. Since an Indian could do as he pleased with a piece of property after receiving a fee patent, he frequently would remove it from sustained-yield management in the case of timberlands, or, with other types of land, withdraw it from inclusion in tribal contracts with various companies for the use or extraction of certain resources.[25]

In October 1957 the BIA conducted a supervised sale of fourteen allotments on the Northern Cheyenne Reservation in southern Montana. The Cheyennes considered at least one of them a key tract since it had a water hole; therefore the tribe wanted to bid on the land. The Tribal Council sold $40,000 worth of cattle to raise the necessary cash, but the bureau delayed the money until it could perform an audit. Moreover, BIA officials refused to postpone the land sale until the funds were available or to allow the tribe to meet the highest bid afterwards. The bureau later called the situation a "mix-up" and maintained that it released the money immediately after learning what it was to be used for, but by then it was too late, and outsiders had made the purchase.[26]

Critics pointed to this episode as evidence that the BIA served the needs of non-Indian westerners rather than the economic livelihood of tribes. After numerous protests, the bureau conducted its own investigation of the affair, but AAIA president Oliver La Farge called it a "whitewash" and accused the Department of the Interior of tolerating "anti-Indian activities" in the BIA. Meanwhile, Emmons again found it necessary to issue reassuring statements to the press in the face of increasing opposition. He declared that he planned to consult with Congress soon on a clarification of policy which would correct "recent misinformation."[27]

# Termination in Action
# and Under Fire

The general decline in sentiment for termination and the increase in the number of Democrats in key policy-making positions in Congress following the 1956 elections also contributed to an increase in the resistance to the two major bills of 1954 affecting the Klamath and Menominee reservations. Moreover, as all of the termination measures were implemented, evidence accumulated that they would devastate both the Indians and the surrounding areas. All of this naturally strengthened the opposition in the fight to change the original laws.

In the case of the Utah Paiutes, for example, the BIA transferred administrative responsibility for the remaining reservation lands to the Walker Bank and Trust Company in Salt Lake City. Controversy soon erupted over the new trustee, partly because of the 160 miles Indians would have to travel to the bank but also because of questionable decisions such as leasing tribal lands to non-Indians for one-fifth the usual price per head. New financial burdens previously assumed by the bureau also strained the budgets of people already living in poverty. Many children found themselves without school lunches because their families could not pay the one-dollar-per-week charge. Health services became nearly unaffordable, and many other unforeseen difficulties arose, including the problem of obtaining welfare payments and old-age assistance from state agencies that required birth certificates as proof of age. Many Indians, of course, had no such documentation.[1]

On the Klamath Reservation, three management specialists chosen by Interior Secretary Douglas McKay were to supervise the division of common property and the subsequent land sales to compensate those members withdrawing from the group and also to report on the future status and operation of the tribe. Eugene C. Favell never played an active role in the committee because of health problems, and after W. L. Phillips resigned to manage McKay's unsuccessful bid for an Oregon senate seat, real estate agent Thomas B. Watters dominated the deliberations. When the group's first reports were completed in 1956, the Senate Committee on Interior and Insular Affairs immediately scheduled hearings in Klamath Falls on the matter. But Republican members protested and refused to attend upon learning that the studies would essentially repudiate the original 1954 bill.[2]

At the hearings Watters revealed that studies performed under contract by the Stanford Research Institute led him to recommend against implementation of the termination act. Investigators polled the Klamaths and estimated that approximately 70 percent would be attracted to the reported $40,000 for each share and elect to withdraw, requiring the sale of about 2.7 billion board-feet of tribally owned timber. The lifting of restrictions on allotments after termination would make another 225 million board-feet available for sale as individual Indians liquidated their assets. Since the law required that timber lands had to be sold by August 13, 1958, approximately 3 billion board-feet of ponderosa pine would go on the area lumber market within a very short time.[3]

The Watters committee concluded that the impact on both the Klamaths and the surrounding area would be profound. The sudden burst in supply would lower prices throughout the entire western pine market, including the amount Indians could expect to receive in sales after termination. Furthermore, the move threatened to put many of the area's smaller logging operations out of business. Without sufficient capital to invest in property, they traditionally relied for much of their source of cutting timber on purchases from Indian land, which would be eliminated if the Klamath forest was sold into private ownership.[4]

Carrying out the law would also damage the environment, according to the studies. The Oregon regulations that would replace BIA sustained-yield forest management after termination required that cutters leave only a few small trees standing. Denuding the area in this fashion would cause considerable erosion damage, harm wildlife habitats, and alter stream flow, which would affect local irrigation districts.[5]

Moreover, Watters told senators at the hearings that the members remaining after termination could not survive as a tribe.

He said that they could not afford taxation and that no form of trusteeship could generate sufficient income because the tribe's forest would be too small after the sales to pay withdrawing members. Studies revealed that the Klamaths also were woefully unprepared for complete termination. Most were undereducated, unfamiliar with life outside the reservation, and unable to fill the many supervisory positions being vacated by the BIA. In addition, there was a lack of unity among the tribe, with off-reservation members caring little about its future and wanting only their financial settlement. Watters recommended federal purchase of the reservation and the leasing of part of it back to the Klamath tribe as the only way to salvage the situation.[6]

Early in 1957 members of the Oregon congressional delegation brought out several proposals, including one that would reimburse the Klamaths for all termination expenses as well as various "stop-gap" measures to delay land sales or to postpone the final implementation of the original act. The antitermination portion of the tribe, led by Boyd Jackson, favored these moves but wanted Congress to go even further in helping nonwithdrawing members to expand their shrunken reservation to support the group better. Many plots of land were already on the open market because the BIA had accelerated the process of fee patenting and supervising sales of trust allotments, especially among heirship lands, to prepare for its exit. Many more holdings would soon appear for sale when tribal property was liquidated, and the remaining Klamaths wanted to buy as much as possible. In this case, the bureau allowed the tribe or an individual Indian to meet the highest bid, but since their loan board had closed along with most others after the recent restriction of Revolving Fund credit, they lacked the money to compete with outsiders.[7]

The faction of Klamaths headed by Wade Crawford, which favored the total liquidation of tribal property, opposed any action that would slow land sales and per-capita distribution. The BIA also objected to the proposals, insisting on a limit to any federal reimbursement of expenses and offering instead a bill that would spread the land sales over a longer period of from four to seven years and thus give Congress a chance to take additional steps it might think necessary.[8]

Under Chairman Neuberger's leadership in the subcommittee, the Senate passed a bill giving the tribe three more years before final termination and allowing up to $1 million to compensate the Indians for the costs. The House subcommittee was less eager to depart from the original bill and forced a 50 percent reduction in the reimbursement figure and a cut in the postponement by one year before approving it. Its report strongly criticized the management specialists for going beyond their assignment and the act's intent by engaging the policy-making activities. Neuberger was dissatisfied with the compromise, but he had to accept the House changes to get the measure to the President for his signature.[9]

Meanwhile, the growing controversy was debated throughout the state in regional newspapers and in meetings of various environmental, church, local government, university, and Indian groups. The conservation-minded magazine *American Forests* began attacking Klamath termination from an ecological point of view in early 1957. Over the next year and a half it carried thirty-two articles on the matter and even encouraged citizen lobbying to amend the act.[10]

In June 1957, for example, William B. Morse of the Wildlife Management Institute described in *American Forests* the importance of the marsh on the Klamath Reservation to the area's ecological system. It not only served as one of the best breeding grounds for wild waterfowl in the entire Pacific flyway, but its ample supply of food and water also aided the area's agriculture. The marsh held the birds for an additional two or three weeks during harvest season, allowing farmers to get all the rice in before the birds migrated south into the fields of the Sacramento and San Joaquin valleys. Morse called for federal purchase of the reservation and conversion of the marsh into a national wildlife refuge.[11]

The next month Mrs. Wade Crawford wrote an article in the same magazine in which she argued that the Klamaths were "Americanized" and that she and others like her wanted nothing to do with the "communistic" tribal government and BIA regulation. As a newly elected member of the tribe's Executive Committee she attacked the management specialists' reports and claimed that the men were incompetent in what they were doing. Mrs. Crawford insisted that individual Indians should have the right to invest their share of tribal property in a place where it could realize a more "sizable capital return on their heritage."[12]

That same summer Senator Neuberger submitted proposal S. 2047 that would authorize the Department of the Interior to buy most of the Klamath Reservation and transfer supervision of the timberlands to the Forest Service and the marshlands to the Fish and Wildlife Service. A three-man appraisal board would determine a fair market value, and the remaining grazing and agricultural lands would be sold on a competitive-bid basis, with preference to tribal members. The Democratic chairman of the Indian Affairs Subcommittee then slated hearings over his bill for early October 1957.[13]

A few witnesses testified at the hearings against federal purchase of the reservation. The Crawford faction demanded implementation of the termination act and the immediate sale of tribal land on a highest-bid basis to guarantee the top price. A representative of one of the area's smaller logging outfits complained that too much land was already under rigid federal control, stifling growth in the industry. The National Lumber Manufacturers Association ignored Neuberger's invitation to participate in the hearings, but it later submitted its views in a letter to the subcommittee and agreed that the reservation should be privately owned.[15]

George Weyerhaeuser of Weyerhaeuser Timber Company, the region's largest firm and a big buyer of timber on Indian land, preferred to retain some regulation. He testified that a sudden increase in the available lumber after termination might encourage new companies to move in or competitors to further expand already overextended capacities. But he also wanted to avoid an extreme departure from the principle of private enterprise and therefore suggested continued government controls after any land transactions or sales, with restrictions included in the deed.[16]

Neuberger's bill received no further congressional attention that session, but the debate began again early the next year. Secretary of the Interior Fred Seaton, who had replaced Douglas McKay after he resigned to run unsuccessfully for an Oregon senate seat, opposed S. 2047 and introduced his own measure, S. 3051, which was similar in some ways to George Weyerhaeuser's ideas. The administration wanted to adhere to its policy of avoiding new federal land acquisitions. The Department of the Interior's proposal therefore would divide the portion of the reservation to be sold into eleven sections large enough to be operated on a

sustained-yield basis and then give private mills the first opportunity to bid on the blocks. The BIA would determine a minimum
price, representing an estimate of what the lands would sell for
in the open market before termination, if 70 percent of the forest
were put up for sale. This measure would protect the Klamaths
at least against the lowest prices the market might reach when
the amount of land for sale suddenly rose. The buyers would also
have to agree to cut the lumber according to a sustained-yield
schedule, and then any timberland not purchased by 1961 would
be bought by the government.[17]

The administration's counterproposal forced Neuberger into a
decision over whether to promote his own bill or Seaton's. He
knew that most of his fellow Western congressmen in key committees were fiscally conservative and would be reluctant to appropriate money to buy the entire reservation; therefore he gave
his support to the Interior measure. The Senate passed the proposal easily, but a battle broke out in the House after lumber
interests began an intense lobbying effort to undermine the sustained-yield cutting restrictions. Al Ullman of Oregon pushed to
substitute the vague phrase "minimum requirements for a continuous supply of timber" for "specifications and minimum
requirements for sustained-yield management" in the Senate version. But the *Oregon Journal* noted that the Democratic representative resisted intense pressure from the area's timber industry
to weak the language even further. Neuberger retaliated aggressively, charging the National Lumber Manufacturers Association
and the Western Pine Association with "staging a blitzkrieg"
against the bill behind closed doors after having refused to appear
in person before any of the hearings on the matter.[18]

In subsequent conference committee proceedings in the summer of 1958, proponents of the House changes contended that
their wording would not impose less stringent forestry standards.
But Ezra Benson, Secretary of the Department of Agriculture
which controlled the Forest Service, called the language so vague
as to invite court tests and encourage wreckless cutting. When
Benson refused to accept responsibility for the reservation unless
his department had full authority to regulate it under the same
sustained-yield provisions as other national forests, the Senate
version prevailed, and conservationists claimed victory.[19]

In the long run the Klamaths would have little reason to cele-
brate. The 77 percent who elected to withdraw from the tribe

received about $43,700 each. Although not all of it was used unwisely, most of the Indians were inexperienced with managing money in the outside world and spent it quickly. Moreover, area businessmen took advantage of the situation and charged the native Klamaths inflated prices for cars, houses, and everything else they sold. The 474 who chose not to leave retained a reservation of about 145,000 acres, which was managed thereafter by the United States National Bank of Portland under trusteeship arrangements. The 617,000 acres to be sold were then divided into eleven blocks and several small, scattered fringe tracts, but private companies bought little of it. The Crown-Zellerbach Corporation later purchased 92,000 acres, and the government eventually paid $68,716,691 to transform four-fifths of the remaining 525,000 acres into the new Winema National Forest and to assign the last one-fifth to the existing Fremont National Forest.[20]

The overwhelming transitional problems in carrying out the Menominee termination bill of 1954 also led to attempts at changing that law. The tribe's rapidly deteriorating financial situation revealed especially the inability of the Indians to survive federal withdrawal. After dispensing the per-capita payment called for in the original act, the Menominees' cash balance dropped from $9,960,895 to $5,075,395. Another distribution resulting from the error in computing annual returns of tribal income to individual members reduced that figure by another $2,000,000. By early 1956 the need to subsidize various services as the BIA withdrew support pushed financial obligations beyond receipts, even though the bureau still financed over $350,000 worth of programs per year.[21]

In addition, the Menominees looked on federal withdrawal with great anxiety and bitterness and doubted their own ability to adjust to the new situation in time to make it alone. They feared the loss of their land through tax delinquency and liens on the holdings of public welfare recipients. There was concern that the Menominee sawmill, the only source of an economic livelihood on the reservation, could not survive when forced to compete with private firms. Few Indians had ever held top management positions, and the operation had always been run like a community co-op, giving more Menominees employment than necessary and not enforcing rigid work habits or a competitive spirit.[22]

The Indians also feared an eventual erosion of tribal status since their termination bill, like all others, gave each member a legally vested right in common property that descended to heirs or could be disposed of under any relevant Wisconsin laws. These individual interests were alienable only according to ordinances passed by the tribe, but the possibility existed that in the future a faction favoring liquidation could come to power in elections and force a partial or total dismemberment of the reservation. Furthermore, since the original bill gave the tribe complete freedom in drawing up a plan for future economic management, there was no stopping certain leaders from allowing quick harvests of the group's timber to the point where the remaining stand could not support the Menominees. Liquidation would then appear to be an attractive alternative. Yet another threat to tribal status came from the state of Wisconsin, which many felt was interested in the reservation's timber. Indian anxiety was only heightened further when, during the 1956 election, the successful candidate for governor declared that the state should purchase the whole reservation.[23]

In the 1956 congressional session, members of the Wisconsin delegation introduced bills that attempted to force changes in the 1954 act. One of the proposals would require a continuation of sustained-yield management restrictions to ensure a constant source of tribal income, another would reimburse the tribe for expenses, and the last one would delay the final termination date until the state could agree with the Menominees on a plan for the future relationship between tribe and state and especially until a lower tax burden could help the Indians financially. The Department of the Interior did not object to federal payment of termination costs, but protested sustained-yield controls as limitations on individual freedom of choice and also strongly disapproved of making BIA withdrawal contingent on any state action. Although Congress approved the sustained-yield requirement and granted federal financing, the 1956 legislative package was still at least a mild setback since the important delay in implementation failed to become law.[24]

When it became clear in early 1957 that the Menominees could not meet the December 31 deadline specified in the original act for submission of a plan for future property management, a tribal delegation went to Washington to try again for an extension. Wisconsin Representative Melvin Laird submitted a measure for a two-year postponement at the Indians' request. When House sub-committee members saw it, they demanded justification. In response, the tribal chairman cited delays by the University of Wisconsin and the state legislature in studying and acting upon various phases in the economic and social integration of the Menominees into the state. Laird convinced the subcommittee to go along, and under his careful leadership the House reported out a bill granting a two-and-one-half-year postponement.[25]

Once in the Senate, however, the proposal fell victim to a dispute between the two subcommittees. Richard Neuberger had recently tried to win federal reimbursement of expenses and a delay in carrying out the termination act affecting the Klamath Indians in his state. The House subcommittee had forced him to accept only 50 percent of government repayment as well as a reduction in the postponement time, and Neuberger now insisted on the same for the Menominees. A conference committee found it impossible to resolve the differences, and Congress adjourned without a bill.[26]

Meanwhile, the tribe continued to struggle with plans for the transition and an existence without the BIA. The Advisory Council led by James G. Frechette, Sr. that had led efforts thus far lacked general support and could not make any moves to deal with the many complex problems. The bureau tried to pressure the Menominees into action by withholding such services as roadwork until the tribe submitted a plan. This tactic only soured relations further. In November 1957 the Indians replaced the Advisory Council with a special Coordinating and Negotiating Committee led by George Kenote, a Menominee who had left the reservation years earlier to work for the BIA; the committee included Mitchell Dodge, Gordon Dickie, and James Frechette, Sr. It began by reviewing the studies that had finally started to come in from the University of Wisconsin, but the reports offered few specific conclusions and therefore left the committee with the task of finding solutions to the many difficult problems.[27]

The University study determined, for example, that the tribe would experience financial and administrative trouble if it formed a separate county. But the Indians as well as nearby non-Indians opposed any merger with an adjoining county. The Menominees feared that they would be outnumbered at the ballot box and thus would be subjected to racial discrimination at the hands of local

government officials and not have any effective political voice.
The new negotiating committee also had the same difficulties as
the Advisory Council in winning the cooperation of increasingly
bitter and reluctant Menominees. The Indians rejected in a referendum all of its proposals to ease the financial crisis by ending
tribal subsidies to various services.[28]

The tribe met the December 31, 1957 deadline for future property management and business organization with only a progress
report. The next year Representative Laird tried again to gain the
legislation that was stalemated the last session by Neuberger's
refusal to let the House give the Menominees anything it had
not granted to the Klamaths. But the Oregon Democrat remained
adamant, and House conferees finally capitulated and accepted
his amendments. As passed in July 1958, the bill authorized the
government to pay half of the Menominees' transitional expenses
and gave the tribe until February 1, 1959 to submit a concrete
plan for future business organization and until August 1, 1959
before final termination.[29]

Meanwhile, the negotiating committee had decided on a type
of voting-trust arrangement to take over the management of the
tribe's sawmill and hired Milwaukee attorney Fred Sammond to
work out the details. It provided for a body of seven trustees to
control the enterprise for at least ten years. This group, which
would make decisions through a simple vote, would have a non-
Indian majority since only three members could be Menominee.
It chose a board of directors, also with a non-Menominee majority, which would elect company officers and determine policy,
while an outsider would be hired as president. An assistance trust
was organized and awarded to the First Wisconsin Trust Company
of Milwaukeee. It received guardian power to act on behalf of minors and those declared legally incompetent. This power enabled
First Trust to control tribal elections since the arrangements applied to 1400 Menominees. Lastly, each tribal member would get
a $3,000 negotiable bond in the business that would pay 4 per-
cent interest and mature in the year 2000, as well as 100 shares
of common stock that would not be negotiable until 1973.[30]

When the tribe met in January 1959 to discuss and vote on the
proposal, heated debate filled the General Council for three days.
Many Indians complained about the degree of outside control
under the plan or the lack of understanding of what it all meant,

and others attacked the entire termination policy. But with the deadline for submitting the draft to the BIA only weeks away, the Menominees decided that it was better than allowing the secretary of the interior to appoint a trustee of his own choice. Therefore they voted to accept the proposal conditionally, pending the enactment of legislation by Wisconsin lawmakers that would guide the integration of the Indians into the state's political and economic structure.[31]

The Wisconsin legislative package, however, encountered considerable opposition. The chairman of the State Senate Committee on Labor, Taxation, Insurance, and Banking, William Trinke, felt that the federal government was trying to shed an unwanted responsibility and had tricked the Menominees. He held up action on the measure for several weeks until Wisconsin's United States senators convinced him that there was no chance for repeal or for amendment of the original termination act. Finally, the legislature passed and the governor signed bills that created a new Menominee County. In a referendum, tribal members had indicated their preference for this solution rather than for a merger with nearby counties. Setting up this political entity became a major concern of the state. More legislation had to be passed making special arrangements for taxation and the performance of some governmental functions by neighboring Shawano County. In what had become a frantic race with time, all of the necessary state laws were completed only two days before the August 1, 1959 deadline.[32]

When the Department of the Interior received the tribal proposal complete with accompanying state legislation, it accepted the draft in principle, but announced it would need time to study and determine if it conformed to the law. The department disliked certain limitations such as the nonnegotiable status of the stock, but it finally certified adoption of the plan in November 1959 after numerous conferences with Menominees and state officials to settle disagreements.[33]

About the same time, tribal elections brought into power new leaders who opposed termination even more intensely than those before. Moreover, the timber market had fallen badly, worsening the financial situation on the reservation. The termination plan had envisioned increased tribal income from heavier lumber cutting to compensate for the loss of BIA subsidies, but the total had actually dropped by about one-half. Unwilling and unable to meet the upcoming final termination date, tribal leaders returned to Washington to plead for more time and more aid. They contended that they needed loans and grants to modernize the sawmill and improve the utility system on the reservation in order to survive.[34]

In 1960 Representative Laird brought out a measure for federal repayment of all termination expenses, exemption from the federal stamp tax on corporation documents, and authority for the secretary of the interior to set a new termination date when he felt the tribe was ready. The bill passed the House but encountered stiff resistance in the Senate, largely because of recent changes in the Indian Affairs Subcommittee. An unsympathetic Frank Church of Idaho became chairman upon the death of Richard Neuberger. Conservatives led by Clinton Anderson of New Mexico began to play a more assertive role after the additions of Barry Goldwater of Arizona and Gordon Allot of Colorado. Senator William Proxmire of Wisconsin became a key spokesman for the tribe, but the subcommittee refused to back away from the basic assumptions and policies of the original act and accused the Menominees of stalling until a later Congress would grant them a longer extension or outright repeal. Therefore, the bill, as passed in September, delayed the final deadline only until April 1961.[35]

Termination took place at that time, but the problems confronting the tribe in implementing the bill and making the transition proved enormous. The tribal sawmill, Menominee Enterprises, Incorporated, had a fifty-year-old facility badly in need of repair, and it shouldered 94 per cent of the county's tax burden. Termination had resulted in the loss of the reservation's school and hospital. Menominee County suffered from the state's worst statistics in employment, education, health, infant mortality, and income. Indians were more likely than other state citizens to rely on hunting and fishing for food, and frequently found themselves in the Shawano jail for violation of state game laws they were now subject to. Menominee anger and discontent only intensified.[36]

# Policy in Retreat

During the last three years of Emmons's term in office, opposition escalated even further. It came not only from white liberals and Native American reformers, but also from a new type of activism based on a resurgent spirit of Indian nationalism that represented in embryonic form the Red Power movement that would emerge as a significant political force on reservations by the 1960s. As the Cold War began to thaw and as the black civil rights movement focused attention on discrimination against minority groups, more and more Native Americans openly rejected assimilation and began to look to their common heritage as a source of strength and ideology. No longer willing to take the political pressure, the Department of the Interior steadily backed away from the policies and principles of the early years of the Eisenhower administration, despite vigorous attempts by Emmons to revive them.

In mid-1957 the commissioner prepared for a new offensive to achieve his policy goals before opponents pushed unwanted legislation through Congress. Any chance of further termination based on the 1954 laws was gone by this time. Senator Arthur Watkins had recently submitted a measure covering the small bands in Michigan, and several California congressmen had introduced proposals involving some groups in their state. They carefully avoided the problems in the unsuccessful attempts three years earlier by guaranteeing prior Indian consent and also by calling for more protection of native rights. But neither measure gained enough support to survive even the Indian affairs subcommittees.[1]

Emmons therefore unveiled a plan that he had been working on for over a year before Secretary of the Interior Fred Seaton and Assistant Secretary Roger Ernst. It would terminate tribes gradually as they were judged ready, with all groups to be removed from federal supervision by July 4, 1976. The date was to coincide with the nation's bicentennial and thus dramatize the theme of liberation and attainment of the full rights and responsibilities of citizenship. Tribes would draw up final rolls and then decide whether to sell or divide group assets or to form some type of corporate entity or trust. Indians over the age of fifteen would get a $100-per-month pension for twelve years or until age sixty-five. BIA appropriations would have to rise for several years to prepare Native Americans for the change, but Emmons maintained that it would ultimately save taxpayers billions of dollars according to projections of future spending levels at the current rate of increase.[2]

To win congressional, public, and Indian backing for the scheme, the commissioner wanted to launch a campaign for support, and he therefore reactivated the American Indian Research Fund (AIRF). This fund has been set up earlier in an unsuccessful attempt to gain financial support from private foundations for reservation resource surveys. Colonel William Ulman of the McCann-Erickson Corporation, the nation's largest public relations firm, agreed to serve as executive secretary of the organization, renamed the American Indian Development Fund (AIDF). Emmons saw it not only as an "educational" device to offset recent criticism, but also as an agency to research and collect materials. Thus, he could use the data to make a presentation before the president in an attempt to win the administration's endorsement of the legislation necessary to implement his ideas.[3]

William W. Keeler, vice-president of Phillips Petroleum Company and chief of the Cherokee Nation, offered to donate $5000 to get the AIDF started and then to use his contacts in the oil industry to solicit more. In January 1958 Ulman and Keeler presented the program to businessmen as a way of implementing the federal withdrawal from Indian affairs expressed in House Concurrent Resolution 108. Before the end of the month, oil and oil-drilling-equipment companies had contributed $6,600, almost all in small sums of from $25 to $250. Emmons and AIDF directors realized the sensitive nature of the fact that all of the money had come from the oil industry and thus naturally did not publicize it.[4]

In early 1958 Ulman approached Lester Norris, a retired oil millionaire with an interest in Indian affairs, and tried to convince him to make a sizable contribution toward a pilot project in Nebraska. Part of Emmons's plan was to link the new termination campaign with the popular theme of reservation industrial development. He wanted the AIDF to perform a human and natural resource survey of the Winnebago Reservation in conjunction with his program of attracting established businesses. He then could promote it, along with the effort to achieve gradual termination for Indians in Nebraska, as a first step in a larger nationwide undertaking. Norris eventually turned over $27,793 worth of stock in the Texas Company to the AIDF to avoid capital-gains taxes.[5]

Meanwhile, the BIA was retreating from its policies on Indian land transactions, which had had as a goal the elimination of trust status and incorporation of native holdings into the system of individual, private tenure that would facilitate the development of reservations primarily by outside entrepreneurs. But many critics preferred tribal development of Indian resources and claimed that the commissioner's policies led to the loss of Indian land through tax default and sales to non-Indians. After protests flooded into the Department of the Interior following the controversial sale of allotments on the Northern Cheyenne Reservation in Montana, Assistant Secretary Roger Ernst ordered changes in bureau regulations in early 1958.[6]

In response, Emmons revoked the infamous "All or None" ruling which he had instituted early in his administration to fee patent as much trust land as possible by requiring a Native American to include all of his property, not just a single plot, when filing a request for a title change. Moreover, the BIA began to allow tribes to meet the highest bid submitted in a supervised sale, unless the owner objected, to give them a better chance to increase their group holdings. It also altered the procedures governing the imposed removal of trust restrictions on allotments belonging to members of the Five Civilized Tribes, which had been authorized under a bill passed in August 1955. The change gave Native Americans an avenue of appeal if the secretary of the interior fee-patented their land without prior consent. An individual could submit a statement within sixty days explaining why he was not sufficiently competent to have trust status lifted. The move was primarily a symbolic concession, however, since officials had not taken any action under the law out of the fear of subsequent objections and criticism.[7]

The BIA still tried to fee-patent trust land within existing regulations but remained sensitive to protest in individual cases. It had recently recommended a proposal to the Indian affairs subcommittees that would repeal acreage restrictions on sales within Montana's Crow Reservation. But when officials announced the opening of bids for May 13, 1958, the Montana congressional delegation demanded an immediate suspension. The BIA agreed to postpone action until Congress had a chance to consider the measure before it that would liberalize transactions on the reservation. The subcommittees killed the bill after the Tribal Council withdrew its approval, and the bureau later rescheduled the sales under its recently revised regulations. Over the next year, similar moratoriums were also imposed on the Standing Rock and Lower Brule reservations in South Dakota and on the Winnebago Reservation in Nebraska. In each case the action came after requests to give tribal councils time to work out land consolidation plans that would permit them to enlarge and improve their group holdings rather than to open up sales to outsiders.[8]

At about the same time, Emmons assigned reservation economic development an even higher priority in response to the heated debate in the summer of 1957 over Senator William Langer's S. 809, which would have provided grants and loans to speed up the industrialization program. Questions had been raised over whether Emmons's approach of attracting established companies was the best of the various alternatives. When the commissioner created the branch of industrial development within the BIA in late 1957, he therefore directed it to reevaluate the effort thus far and to make recommendations. To no one's surprise, the subsequent investigation reaffirmed Emmons's method, and the bureau then expanded its program and merely tried to correct a few past problems.[9]

Emmons added Noel Sargent, for example, a consultant who had worked in several top staff positions for the National Association of Manufacturers, to the BIA's industrialization program. He also placed specialists in bureau area offices in Phoenix, Arizona; Aberdeen, South Dakota; Gallup, New Mexico; Anadarko, Oklahoma; Minneapolis, Minnesota; and Portland, Oregon to draw up reservation fact sheets on such matters as the potential labor force, transportation facilities, and available resources. The commissioner then created field offices in manufacturing areas to serve as points of contact with industrialists. The first one opened in Los Angeles in late 1957 under D. E. Whelan, and additional offices soon followed in Cleveland, Denver, and St. Louis.[10]

Despite these efforts, Native American pressure on Congress and the BIA to do even more only increased, especially among groups on the northern plains where Indian economies were the most devastated. In 1958, the third annual Conference on Indian Problems at Northern Montana College resolved that the government should act quickly to stimulate further reservation development. At about the same time, Montana's Intertribal Policy Board petitioned the bureau to enlarge its program. Joseph Garry, a Coeur d'Alene member of the Idaho legislature, led a National Congress of American Indians (NCAI) delegation that same year on a visit to Puerto Rico. The government had recently undertaken a massive project, "Operation Bootstrap," to attract industry to the commonwealth with tax breaks and other incentives. The experience reaffirmed Garry's belief that the answer was more technical aid and a low-interest loan program from the BIA. It also gave the NCAI another opportunity to link the issue of assistance to Indians with that of help to underdeveloped peoples outside of the states.[11]

The BIA negotiated with Sears, Roebuck and Company in 1958 to place a bureau representative in its Chicago office who would work with the firm's 400 buyers in finding prospective industries to locate near reservations among the thousands of manufacturers that produced for Sears. The commissioner accelerated his personal campaign to interest businessmen in the program and distributed a press release entitled "New Indian Program Interests Industry" to approximately eighty trade journals with the request that they publish it. He also wrote articles for business magazines to popularize the effort and to urge corporate participation.[12]

Meanwhile, congressional opponents of BIA policies carried on their efforts to expand the government commitment, despite the failure of S. 809 the previous year. In 1958 Senator Paul Douglas of Illinois led another drive for a bill to stimulate industrialization in depressed regions of the country to reverse the economic recession. He again included Indian areas in his measure. In a significant recognition of reservations as legal and political entities, the Area Redevelopment Act (ARA) would allow tribes, as well as states and their subdivisions, to receive grants and loans for land acquisition or development, the construction of basic pub-

lic service facilities, or industrialization projects. Congress passed
the ARA in the late summer of 1958, but President Eisenhower
vetoed the bill as unnecessary and inflationary.[13]

At the same time, Emmons and AIDF directors were moving
ahead with plans to launch a pilot project in Nebraska as part of
their continuing campaign for a program of gradual termination,
coupled with an effort to attract outside industry. The BIA worked
out the details of termination proposals in mid-1958 and intended
to send everything to the AIDF for its use in a planning conference to be held on July 15, 1958, between executive secretary
Colonel William Ulman, bureau officials, and representatives
from the University of Nebraska. Ulman stoody ready to contract
with Communications Counselors, Incorporated, and Market
Planning Corporation, both subsidiaries of the McCann-Erickson
complex, to execute the studies and handle the public relations
drive to gain the support of Indians as well as the general public
for the idea.[14]

But when Assistant Interior Secretary Roger Ernst heard news
of the meeting several weeks before the scheduled date, he immediately withheld any BIA materials from being sent to the
AIDF. By this time anything even resembling termination evoked
intense opposition, which the Department of the Interior preferred to avoid. In a letter to the commissioner, Ernst noted the
"rather hysterical report we received from the Omaha Tribal
Council" and stated that he had ordered the Nebraska conference
called off.[15]

Another indication that the Department of the Interior was
backing away from its position in the battle over how to develop
reservations came in mid-1958 when the BIA began wavering in
its opposition to the addition of new lands to tribal holdings. Various congressmen frequently submitted bills at the request of Indian constituents that would give tribes title to either undisposed
surplus lands remaining after Dawes Act cessions or submarginal
lands which went unclaimed under homesteading laws. The latter lands had been bought by the government in the 1930s under
the National Industrial Recovery Act and used thereafter by Indians or administered for their benefit. Throughout Emmons's
term in office, the BIA had blocked these measures, except in a
few instances where they could be used to extract tribal acceptance of a termination plan.[16]

The bureau's opposition had been based on the principle of integrating Indian land into the dominant system of tenure rather than increasing the acreage under restrictive title. But the experience of some Native Americans revealed that pressure from nearby non-Indians could also be a factor. Various Pueblo tribal leaders, for example, had tried for years to win congressional approval of a measure giving them title to certain submarginal lands surrounding their homes. In 1956 the BIA had diluted one such proposal before submitting it to the subcommittees. The bureau altered the legislation to give tribal councils merely the right to buy up leasing permits held by outsiders as they expired so as not to disturb long-time lease holders. It did not pass even in that form, but after the bureau began to ease its resistance to tribal land acquisitions, bills were successfully enacted in 1958 which not only covered the Pueblos but also the Coeur d'Alene reservation in Idaho, the Spokane reservation in Washington, and the Crow and Fort Peck reservations in Montana.[17]

By the fall of 1958 the retreat from previous policies had gone so far that the Department of the Interior was ready to issue an important symbolic gesture to indicate the change. In September Secretary Fred Seaton gave a speech at the Navajo agency in Window Rock, Arizona that was broadcast over the radio to all Indians of the area. He acknowledged the recent controversy surrounding the "differing interpretations of House Concurrent Resolution 108" and stated that hereafter no group would lose federal services or supervision unless it clearly demonstrated that it was fully prepared and understood and supported the action.[18]

Despite the recent drift away from strict conservative principles in Indian policy, the sudden move came as a surprise and threw the BIA into confusion for a short time. Some officials questioned how they should proceed at this point, realizing that Seaton's speech implied a complete turnaround in the bureau's dealings with tribes by guaranteeing prior consent over actions affecting them. In response, Emmons merely reiterated his own support of the federal withdrawal from Indian affairs outlined in Resolution 108 and said he would issue further instructions after receiving clarification of the secretary's remarks. There was soon little doubt, however, concerning Seaton's intentions after the Department of the Interior repudiated the resolution as an immediate goal and the BIA started advertising the September speech as "one of the most important developments of the year."[19]

Nevertheless, critical press coverage and attacks on administration programs continued, especially by television reporters as networks devoted more attention to government policies and conditions among Native Americans. In 1958 a well-known local TV announcer in San Francisco, Don Sherwood, described a very bleak situation of poverty and death on the Navajo Reservation and appealed to viewers for action. Emmons and Navajo Tribal Chairman Paul Jones rushed to appear on Sherwood's show to refute the story, but an even more controversial report soon followed.[20]

In the fall of 1958 reporter and news commentator Edward R. Murrow had expressed the hope in one of his popular television appearances that all of what he referred to as the "phoney Hollywood Indians" would soon be killed off so TV could pay some attention to the plight of the real ones. Murrow's words were widely noticed and inspired the National Broadcasting Company (NBC) to run a hard-hitting documentary on November 16 entitled "The American Stranger" as an episode in its "Kaleidoscope" series. The program described wretched conditions throughout the West and showed revealing scenes of the Blackfoot, Flathead, Navajo, and Menominee reservations. Moreover, it attacked various BIA actions such as the pressure on the Menominees to accept termination, the controversial 1957 land sale on the Northern Cheyenne Reservation, and the land and credit policies that contributed to the constant loss of Indian property. The Department of the Interior immediately retaliated with a thirty-one-page rebuttal to the broadcast in which it attacked NBC for not adequately emphasizing the bureau's positive achievements. It blamed Indian problems on segregation, a tradition of paternalism, and "surplus population," but the damage had already been done.[21]

As 1958 came to a close, the BIA made several additional changes that indicated it was modifying its commitment to the administration's original policies and conceding more to opponents in the battle over reservation development. It made a $500,000 grant available in December from the Revolving Fund Credit program for a project to consolidate tribal holdings on the segmented Rosebud Reservation in South Dakota through a series of purchases and exchanges. The bureau also promised to finance a similar effort soon on the Pine Ridge Reservation in the same state.[22]

In addition, the BIA announced at about the same time an increase in loan programs to help Alaska Indians modernize fishing fleets. This came largely in response to a congressional investigation a year earlier that had severely criticized the restriction of credit in Alaska and the recent bureau attempts to interest outside firms in buying out Indian cooperative canneries there. In another, primarily symbolic, move, the Department of the Interior started issuing executive renewals of trust status on allotments under the Dawes Act that would extend for five years rather than one year, the renewal period used since 1951.[23]

Despite the recent retreat in many areas, the BIA continued its effort to bring factories to reservations, but with diminishing success. By this time arrangements under the program were relatively standard. Tribes usually financed the construction of a building, but contracts with companies now required a monthly fee from firms to repay the investment. At the end of the contract period, which was most often twenty years, the company became the owner of the facility.[24]

In 1959, a California manufacturer negotiated a contract with the BIA and the Confederated Tribes of the Umatilla Reservation in Oregon. A few years earlier Congress had passed a bill allowing the government to transfer title to lands and buildings that had been used in the construction of various flood-control projects to Indians for the purpose of attracting industry. The Umatilla tribe took advantage of the law and received the McNary Dam townsite in Oregon to offer the company in return for locating near the reservation. Before the end of the year, about forty Native Americans had found employment making mobile homes in the new plant.[25]

One of the BIA's new field industrial development specialists contacted officials of Harn Enterprises that same year and discussed their establishing a branch on the Cherokee Reservation in North Carolina. During subsequent negotiations, the Tribal Council agreed to spend $150,000 of its own money and an equal sum borrowed from the bureau to build a factory, the first of its kind to be constructed entirely by Indian resources. The BIA entered into a contract with the company for on-the-job training subsidies, and in late 1959 the plant started turning out quilting products and other related items.[26]

The AIDF also continued to promote Emmons's industrialization program but of course had to drop its accompanying campaign for termination. It turned once again to an effort to finance reservation resource surveys as a prelude to private development and used money previously donated by oil millionaire Lester Norris to contract with the Massachusetts Institute of Technology (MIT) for a study of the Rosebud and Pine Ridge reservations in South Dakota. MIT professors, led by Everett E. Hagen in economics and Louis C. Schaw in social psychology, performed the work and ultimately published a report entitled *The Sioux on the Reservation.* The study proved of little value, however, since it concentrated more on cultural and personality traits that discouraged economic initiative among Indians than on the potential economic development of the reservations.[27]

Congressional attempts to expand the BIA's program to stimulate reservation economies even further also increased in 1959 but failed in each case. Senator William Langer of North Dakota brought out a measure similar to his S. 809 of two years earlier, authorizing loans and grants to tribes, individual Indians, or non-Indians who fulfilled the purpose of the act. Once again the proposal failed to make it out of committee. Forces led by Democrats promoted another Area Redevelopment Act which included tribes as recipients of grants and loans for industrialization projects and public service facilities attractive to companies. The outcome was the same as the year before; Congress passed the proposal and President Eisenhower vetoed it.[28]

Representative E. Y. Berry of South Dakota promoted a bill referred to as "Operation Bootstrap," which he said resulted from the recent visit by a NCAI delegation to Puerto Rico. The proposal amounted to an attempt to attract industries to reservations with a ten-year tax exemption. The Department of the Interior would approve the scheme only if it was changed to include wage standards and a way of preventing marginal enterprises from coming and then leaving when tax breaks ran out. Ironically, these stipulations were very similar to complaints previously levied against the BIA's own program.[29]

Some support for the bill came from northern plains tribes, which were so desperate for aid that they did not strongly resist outside penetration. Extensive allotment during the past century had rendered many groups there fragmented and loosely bound by organizational structure or tradition. Other Indians were concerned about the lack of tribal control over the program and demanded consent over any companies locating on their reservations. Compared to previous stimulative measures, the bill found only lukewarm support. It did not reach the full Congress in 1959 and failed again the following year when Berry had reintroduced it.[30]

Even more important in the long term, a growing rejection of assimilation and a related emergence of political activism based on Indian nationalism also became increasingly evident in 1959. Early in the year a faction of very traditional and anti-BIA Native Americans came to power in the Iroquois Council House in New York. Recent controversies in the state over taxation and condemnation of lands for flood-control projects had angered many Indians. The government intended, for example, to inundate much of the Seneca Reservation in the construction of the Kinzua Dam on the Allegheny River. The Indians claimed that the unilateral seizure of their property would violate the Pickering Treaty of 1794, but federal officials no longer considered treaties enforceable and maintained that the right of eminent domain superseded any centuries-old agreement. Despite numerous protests and interventions by some New York authorities, including Governor Averell Harriman, the Senecas lost every court appeal in the defense of their homelands.[31]

In early March, Herbert C. Holdridge, a retired army general who had been a classmate of President Eisenhower's at West Point, launched a campaign to help the Iroquois. His unusual political organizations and crusades and his habit of writing very hostile letters to public officials on a number of issues had led many to consider him somewhat eccentric. He believed that sensational techniques were necessary to draw attention to injustices, especially in the case of federal Indian policy. The general felt that tribes were legitimate and sovereign entities, and he fully supported Indian nationalists and traditionalists in the fight against assimilation and federal encroachment on their lands.[32]

On March 19, 1959, Holdridge and about a hundred Iroquois, together with a few western Indians, marched on the White House and demanded a conference with President Eisenhower. Officials did not let the demonstrators in, but said they would refer the matter to the Department of the Interior. The next day a smaller group appeared at Emmons's office, charged the commissioner with "permitting crimes against Indians," and announced that they intended to put him under citizen's arrest. Emmons naturally refused to come out, and for the next few days the Washington police kept his office and home under surveillance.[33]

By now the established opposition was beginning to see changes away from extreme termination and withdrawal in recent administration policy. Therefore they denounced the sensational confrontation tactics and kept their distance from the protestors. The NCAI resolved against such demonstrations at its 1959 convention, and in a surprising reflection of the thaw in relations, it also presented Emmons with a citation for services to Indians. Even one of the BIA's oldest and harshest critics, Harold Fey of the *Christian Century*, attacked this dramatic way of trying to achieve reform.[34]

Nevertheless, activities by Indian nationalists became even more widespread. In early April 1959 representatives of many tribes, including Miccosukee Seminoles, Onondagas, Tuscaroras, Mohawks, Senecas, and Chippewas, met in the Florida Everglades and signed a buckskin to symbolize their approval of a plan to form a united Indian nation. Later that same month General Holdridge went to the Navajo Reservation, where political factionalism had recently increased after tribal elections. The most traditional and anti-BIA Navajos had opposed the reelection of chairman Paul Jones and tried to nominate Raymond Nakai to run against him. When that failed, they planned to vote for Nakai as a write-in candidate, but the bureau would not allow it. Jones won the contest and the disaffected Navajos charged voting fraud, as they had in every election for years.[35]

To Holdridge this was a perfect example of how the BIA violated treaties and Indian autonomy by conducting elections in a way that guaranteed the victory of leaders who were pliable "puppets." In early April he and a few supporters distributed posters around the reservation with pictures of Eisenhower and Emmons, calling for their arrest for offenses against Indians. Early on the morning of April 21, 1959, the general and four or five Navajos appeared at Paul Jones's home, where Holdridge called the chairman out and read a statement which purported to put him under citizen's arrest and also declared the recent elections null and void. Jones, of course, refused to cooperate, and the incident ended for the time being.[36]

Over the next few days, Holdridge continued to agitate on behalf of Jones's opponents. He called for a mass meeting on May 3
near the Window Rock agency to outline the charges against the
chairman, but before it could take place, law enforcement officials entered into the case of the attempted arrest of Jones. The
general had demonstrated his ability to mobilize Indian anti-BIA
sentiment and draw attention to a subject that was troublesome
for the administration, and the government wanted his activities
stopped. The area's U.S. attorney, the Navajo Tribal Police, the
Department of Justice, and the solicitor of the Department of the
Interior all worked together to find a charge that could apply to
the situation. After considering charges of malicious mischief,
criminal libel, and false imprisonment, a bureau deputy special
officer finally arrested Holdridge on May 2. He charged the general with assaulting Jones because he had allegedly prevented him
from moving by placing his hand on his shoulder while reading
the list of accusations.[37]

Several days after the general's capture, United States attorney
Jack D. H. Hays entered a motion into the Arizona District Court
that he be examined by a psychiatrist. Results of the subsequent
tests were never announced but must have been negative since
Holdridge eventually stood trial in Prescott, Arizona and was
aquitted of assault charges on November 13, 1959. The incident,
however, prompted the formation of the Dineh Rights Association, which quickly gained about a thousand Navajo supporters.
It continued to agitate for election reform and also provided an
organizational structure for the opposition to Chairman Jones.
The association held that more of the tribe's income should be
used to alleviate poverty on the reservation and less for the projects
to attract industry recently promoted by the BIA and Jones.[38]

Throughout the remainder of Emmons's term in office, Indian
activists continued their protests and demonstrations. At the
same time they gained an increased awareness of their own unique
historic heritage, largely as a result of the influence of the black
civil rights movement. In 1959 the Rosebud Sioux Tribal Council took advantage of the Civil Rights Act of 1957 and filed complaints of discrimination with the new Civil Rights Commission
set up under the law. The South Dakota Indians maintained that
they were routinely excluded from juries, were more likely to receive stiff sentences for crimes than non-Indians, and experienced

discrimination in schools and other state institutions. Moreover, in meetings at Oklahoma City in February 1960 and at Fort Gibson, Oklahoma the following June, delegates from many tribes assembled to protest television's distortions of their past. They demanded that TV portray their struggle to defend homelands rather than picture them as savages who plundered and killed needlessly.[39]

At about the same time, representatives of the Hopi tribe, which had always been very traditional and anti-BIA, took their protests against the government's violation of their sovereignty to the United Nations. They drove across the country and pleaded with officials of foreign countries to help them stop the recent development of oil and coal on their land and the Defense Department's plans to put a bombing range just south of where they lived. In July 1960 a delegation of Chippewas went to the United Nations and requested membership on the basis of the sovereignty recognized in their treaty. Several months later a faction of Utes on the Uintah and Ouray Reservation in Utah who called themselves the "True Utes" issued a declaration of secession from the United States following a long-standing feud with the government over a land cession in northeastern Utah.[40]

The recent surge of Indian nationalism and its effect on BIA policy were also reflected in negotiations between the bureau and the Miccosukee Seminoles of Florida, one of the nation's most fiercely independent tribes. The 545 members of this group considered themselves an unconquered, sovereign nation still at war with the United States since they had never signed a treaty of surrender or ceded any land. They rejected the limitations of reservations assigned to them in the early twentieth century and refused to associate with the Muskogee band of Seminoles which had accepted life under BIA supervision. Although some Miccosukees had become part of the reservation group, most continued to roam the Everglades along the Tamiami Trail in search of fish and game as they had for over a century, but recent economic development by cattlemen and oil companies in the region threatened their life-style.[41]

Realizing that they had to act to halt further encroachment, the Indians sent a "buckskin declaration" to the White House as early as 1954 in which they outlined their grievances and requested that the administration send a representative to negotiate. Emmons went to Florida that fall, but he accomplished little because the Miccosukees claimed more land that he was willing to allow them. They also demanded federal recognition, which the BIA would not concede since it would imply an aid commitment at a time the bureau was trying to reduce its responsibilities and expenditures.[42]

Talks resumed in late 1955 and narrowed the differences over the land issue considerably. Since the area in question belonged to Florida and not to the federal government, Emmons then appeared before the state's governor and his cabinet early the next year and convinced them to set aside 200,000 acres for the "perpetual and exclusive use" of the Indians. But negotiations broke down again after the Miccosukees split among themselves over the issues of state takeover of law-and-order jurisdiction and the education of children in public schools.[43]

By this time the general drive for quick termination and withdrawal from Indian affairs had faltered, and Emmons was willing to recognize another tribal organization. But rather than accept the Miccosukee leadership, he tried to isolate them and draw all Seminoles into a more controllable body. The commissioner checked into the background of the Miccosukees' lawyer, Morton Silver, and claimed he was an ex-Communist who was merely trying to use Indian issues as a source of political agitation. In early 1957 he instructed the BIA to assist the Muskogee faction, also known as the Reservation Seminoles, in drawing up an IRA charter and constitution. The bureau then invited all Seminoles to join, in hopes that many Miccosukees would participate since only this recognized group would receive income from leases on tribal land.[44]

But most Miccosukees rejected these arrangements and, instead, appealed to the governor and the state Indian commissioner for recognition and the exclusive use of a portion of any lands given to the Seminoles. In the summer of 1957 the governor granted their request and tried to work out a division of the area previously offered between the two factions. This effort failed, however, because the Miccosukees insisted on either outright ownership of the land or a perpetual trusteeship, while the Florida officials demanded a recapture clause that would allow them to force the return of the land if they deemed it necessary at some future date to ensure ultimate state control and future economic development of the area.[45]

Emmons returned to Florida in early 1958 to try to bring the state and the Indians together. In a further reflection of the BIA's retreat from previous policies, he extended federal recognition to the Miccosukees. But he was careful to explain that the action implied no BIA responsibility toward them. The commissioner then promoted a scheme whereby the Indians would receive in trust the campsites used in their traditional migration along the Tamiami Trail, and the state would retain control over the rest of the reservation. But the Miccosukees still insisted on at least a perpetual trust over all the area.[46]

In the fall of 1958 the Indians resorted to the tactics currently gaining widespread use among activists. A group of Miccosukees traveled to Washington and took their grievances before the British, French, and Spanish embassies. Early the next year they attracted even more attention in New York by publicly threatening to take their case to the United Nations. Several of the Indians even appeared on an NBC television talk show hosted by Dave Garroway. Emmons was also a guest on the same program and tried to emphasize Florida's responsibility in the affair. Nevertheless, the entire incident had an impact which the commissioner later called "most unfortunate."[47]

This type of activity suddenly made the state very reluctant to deal with the Miccosukees. A five-man committee appointed by Governor LeRoy Collins declared that the Indians were a minority who were attracting public attention out of proportion to their numbers through "white men's promotional tactics." Then, just as the BIA had tried earlier, Florida officials attempted to isolate the Miccosukees. They brought out a plan in August of 1959 that would retain ultimate state authority but give the Indians exclusive use of the area "as long as the Seminole Indians are residing in Florida" and that would posit administrative control with the Muskogee faction.[48]

The state also requested that the BIA extend additional aid to the Indians under their plan. Emmons was ready by this time to concede at least a few additional services. But surprisingly, he now insisted that Florida first agree to arrangements drawn up by the two factions that would divide the reservation and allow the Miccosukees to remain independent and control their own land. The state still considered this unacceptable and offered a counterproposal to lease the area to the bureau if it would clear more grazing land, construct sewage systems, and provide a part-time official to help the Miccosukees in a development effort. But this was still more than the BIA was willing to undertake, and Florida finally acted on its own. Governor Collins backed away from his firm position against giving the Miccosukees independent control over a separate tract and on April 5, 1960 permitted the Florida Board of Commissioners of State Institutions to make 143,620 acres available for the exclusive use of the Trail Indians in their traditional way. The state retained ultimate control, granting revocable land-use licenses after individual Seminoles submitted plans for development. This fell short of the original demand for outright ownership, and one very traditional faction under Ingraham Billie refused to have any part of the proposal.[49]

But most of the affected Miccosukees at last reluctantly accepted the arrangements, and over the subsequent years the tribe's position improved even though it had not attained the total sovereignty that many had insisted upon. In 1962 the secretary of the interior officially recognized the Miccosukees as an entity separate and independent from the rest of the Seminoles. Federal recognition also made the Miccosukees eligible for government aid, including schools, housing, and low-income programs such as Head Start. Perhaps most important, the tribe gained an unusual degree of control over its own destiny by establishing a contract relationship with the BIA in which funds were transferred from the bureau to a tribal non-profit corporation that handled expenditures, allowing the Miccosukees to run all their own programs.[50]

# 10

# Conclusion

Federal Indian policy has largely followed the vacillations of national politics throughout American history. Perhaps the most important determinant has been the ebb and flow of U.S. cultural and expansionistic nationalism, which clashes directly with Native American sovereignty and cultural autonomy.

Following World War II, resurgent conservatism growing out of the reaction against Franklin D. Roosevelt's liberalism, the economic boom stimulated in part by the availability of new markets in America's recently acquired global empire, and the nationalism engendered by the wartime experience set the stage for the most intense assault on Indian sovereignty in the twentieth century. The election of Dwight D. Eisenhower and a Republican congressional majority in 1952 gave western terminationists the opportunity to set in motion policies based on their conservative ideology. They envisioned a narrowly defined American culture and saw liberty and freedom as simply the opportunity to compete individually within the nation's dominant economic institutions in the absence of any government involvement. Eisenhower appointed a New Mexican banker, Glenn Emmons, to head the BIA and implement the new policies, partly as a reward for his help in delivering New Mexico in the presidential election and partly because he adhered to the conservative, businessman's viewpoint.

The new administration's first moves involved trying to dismantle the BIA by reducing its budget and transferring some of its functions to other government agencies, removing as much land as possible from trust status, and terminating the federally recognized tribal status upon which much of the remaining Indian culture and sovereignty rested. But each action only fueled an escalating opposition. Liberals were appalled at the human consequences of budget reductions and the withdrawal of federal responsibility from some of the neediest people in America. Local government officials feared inheriting the financial burden of poverty-stricken Indians. Native American groups and their non-Indian allies attacked programs which they saw as destroying the Indian land base, denying Indian culture and sovereignty, and ignoring Indian opinion. And in some cases environmentalists joined the opposition out of the fear that the dismemberment of reservations would harm the ecology.

In the meantime, Commissioner Emmons tried to disarm the opposition. He publicized a "three-prong attack" on the problems faced by reservations and conducted nationwide conferences to suggest an Indian voice in making policy. In the face of growing demands for a greater federal commitment in stimulating Indian economies through tribal enterprises that would retain native culture and sovereignty, he promoted a program of industrial development with little government involvement, led by outside—and inevitably white—businessmen.

But by the late 1950s these defensive moves were overwhelmed by an opposition generated by a rising Indian nationalism that coincided with the recent movement toward minority and ethnic consciousness and by a general retreat from extreme conservative politics in the country. The Department of the Interior gradually forced the BIA to back away from termination policies so as to save face. Hence Emmons never fully realized his goals as a terminationist commissioner. Although he looked with pride upon such accomplishments as the transfer of health services to the Department of Health, Education, and Welfare, the adult education program, and the placement of many more Navajo children in schools, Native Americans were still not integrated into the dominant culture and its institutions, and the general direction of Indian policy set in the 1930s by John Collier's "Indian New Deal" was not significantly reversed.[1] The lack of success was due in part to broader trends in national politics, but also to dissatisfaction with the dramatic change and dislocation in tribal life threatened by the policies of the 1950s. Relocation disrupted the social fabric of reservations and contributed to the burgeoning of Indian urban slums which made Native American poverty even more visible than it was on isolated reservations. Programs to standardize patterns of land tenure, and to place more children in public schools, as well as economic development led by non-Indian industrialists and termination of Indian Reorganization Act (IRA) charters seemed to destroy any notion of independent sovereignty by eroding the foundation of cultural distinction and by shifting control of tribal destiny to people and institutions outside the Indian community.

After ending his service as commissioner, Emmons continued to promote the scheme of termination that he had devised in 1956 when it became clear that the tribe-by-tribe legislative approach of the earlier 1950s would fail. In fact, he began writing a book in which he once again spelled out a plan of gradual termination that would culminate with the nation's bicentennial on July 4, 1976. As groups were terminated, Indians over fifteen would receive $100 per month for twelve years or until age sixty-five in order to phase in the change and make the transition less abrupt. The book was never finished or published, but its proposed title, *Freedom for the First Americans*, reflected Emmons's continuing adherence to the "liberation" view of termination and to federal withdrawal from Indian affairs. He believed that ultimately the issue involved achieving the "full rights and responsibilities of citizenship."[2]

Because the controversial policies of the 1950s stimulated intense opposition well before the end of Emmons's term in office, the transition toward a new phase of federal Indian policy began several years before the Democrats swept the Republicans out of office in the 1960 elections. Then in January of that year, just as President-elect John F. Kennedy was organizing his new administration, the Fund for the Republic published the results and conclusions of the study of Indian affairs it had initiated in 1957. The study attacked the Republican policies of withdrawal and termination and recommended a shift toward more economic development of reservations and greater Indian participation in decisions affecting them. Six months later a group of Native American leaders issued a "Declaration of Indian Purpose," which also repudiated recent policies, and demanded a greater tribal role in their own affairs.[3]

The new secretary of the interior, Stewart Udall, immediately set out to make changes and secured the appointment of an anthropologist, Philleo Nash, as the next commissioner of Indian Affairs. He also ordered a study by a special task force. Like the report issued by the Fund for the Republic, of which Udall had been a part, this study called for more reservation development and Indian self-control.[4]

The policies of the 1960s still reflected some of the patterns established during the previous decade, but nonetheless the federal government accepted a greater role in reservations, and "Indian self-determination" became the new catch-phrase, although there was disagreement over how it should be achieved. In 1962 the BIA organized a Division of Economic Development in accordance with recent recommendations. Despite the fact that only six small plants remained in operation at the end of Emmons's term in office, most subsequent industrialization efforts followed the pattern he set in trying to make reservations more appealing to outside business. The Area Redevelopment Act and the Economic Development Act in the 1960s provided grants and loans to stimulate Indian economies. Together with increased bureau activity, they helped attract 137 factories before the end of the decade.[5]

Various public works projects that became available in 1962 under the Manpower Development Training Act directly employed many Native Americans. In addition, Indians participated in some of President Lyndon Johnson's Great Society programs such as Upward Bound, Job Corps, and Community Action, and many government agencies outside the BIA thus became involved in reservation rehabilitation. Major policy reversals were limited only by the presence of many congressmen on the Indian affairs subcommittees who still favored some type of termination and federal withdrawal. The relocation program continued, although the name was changed to Employment Assistance, and more emphasis was placed on job training.[6]

Some economic and social progress resulted, but it came more slowly than hopes and expectations. Confrontation and militancy consequently replaced less dramatic attempts at reform with greater frequency. The Red Power movement of course mirrored the same surge of activism that occurred throughout the nation in the 1960s involving other groups and issues. In November 1969, Native Americans occupied Alcatraz Island in San Francisco Bay in an act of protest. In 1972, Indians conducted a Broken Treaties Caravan to Washington, D.C., and a few destroyed large quantities of records in the BIA building. In the most sensational act, the following year militants seized the village of Wounded Knee, South Dakota, site of an 1890 massacre of Sioux by the U.S. Seventh Cavalry, to dramatize mistreatment over the years.[7]

All of this occurred at the same time that at least some progress was being made in the direction of self-determination. In a special message to Congress in 1970, President Richard Nixon repudiated termination and spoke in favor of Indian control over reservations. The crowning achievement came in 1975 with the passage of the Indian Self-Determination Act, which gave tribes a significant role in setting policy goals and in administering all federal programs affecting them.[8]

The most dramatic example of rejection and reversal of termination was the restoration of the Menominee reservation in Wisconsin. Throughout the 1960s after the bill terminating the Menominees took effect, problems stemming from that action became increasingly evident. With the tribal sawmill, Menominee Enterprises, Inc. (MEI), serving as virtually the entire tax base for the new county, the Menominees soon found themselves unable to handle the full burden of social services, and they had to rely more heavily than ever upon federal and state tax dollars. Discontent among the Indians over termination had been high from the beginning, but it intensified and became organized in the late 1960s. Local discrimination, especially in public schools, was one central issue. Even more important was a decision by the voting trust that managed the former reservation and was dominated by non-Menominees to create a multiseason tourist complex around beautiful West Lake and to sell vacation plots to outsiders. Supporters saw it as a necessary measure to bring in more money and expand the tax base, but opponents considered it the final outrage and initiated a grassroots movement known as the Determination of Rights and Unity for Menominees (DRUMS).[9]

Organized protests began in 1970. President Nixon's statements against termination then encouraged DRUMS to broaden its opposition to include termination itself and to begin working for a reversal of the bill that had ended their tribal status. In March 1972 a Menominee delegation journeyed to Washington, and with the help of LaDonna Harris, Philleo Nash, and the Robert Kennedy Youth Project, they formed the National Committee to Save the Menominee People and Forest to work for restoration of the reservation. Wisconsin senators William Proxmire and Gaylord Nelson introduced the necessary legislation in April 1972; in an unprecedented move both houses of Congress overwhelmingly passed it, and President Nixon signed the bill on December 22, 1973. Trust status was regained and a new constitution created as the basis for tribal government.[10]

As Native Americans and their tribal institutions made gains, however, non-Indian westerners frequently became alarmed and organized a reaction. In 1976 the Interstate Congress for Equal Rights and Responsibilities, composed primarily of whites within or near reservations, formed to agitate on issues ranging from the status of certain lands to political control of areas with heavy Indian population and the nontaxable status of Native American property. Congressmen introduced various bills to abrogate all treaties and thus end the recent spate of court actions initiated by Indians to reclaim lands; to increase state control over law-and-order jurisdiction; and to eliminate Indian water rights.[11]

Native Americans were more politically organized by this time. In the summer of 1978 activists protested the most recent threats to Indian sovereignty by marching across the country to Washington, D.C., in what became known as "The Longest Walk." They thus were able to forestall, at least for a time, what they saw as simply another termination attempt.[12]

But the early 1980s revealed that the struggle was far from over. National politics again became very conservative, and forces were emerging reminiscent of those that stimulated the controversial policies of the 1950s. A nationalistic Republican, Ronald Reagan, came to the presidency determined to cut federal expenditures, especially in social programs that traditionally aid the most needy and disadvantaged. He brought with him a commitment to unfettered industrial development under the leadership of private business and, correspondingly, support for the increasing cries, epitomized in the "Sagebrush Rebellion," to open up federally controlled western lands to private ownership and development.

However the political pendulum swings in the future, the nation will continue to struggle with several difficult problems that have developed over the course of relations between Indians and the U.S. Conflicting sovereignty, for example, involves the status of the competing political entities and the question of whether treaties are still binding. Contradictory principles have become embodied in policies, legislation, and even court decisions. The related issue of dual citizenship arising from the retention of at least some tribal sovereignty together with the 1924 act granting U.S. citizenship is another perplexing dilemma. The questions of how reservations should be developed economically and how to deal with the social and cultural dislocation that industrialization brings also demand resolution. And last, if tribal self-determination is the accepted choice, then a decision-making process must be firmly established to make it a stable and genuine doctrine, in order to avoid the undue intrusion of considerations and pressures that arise outside reservations.

# Notes

## Abbreviations

American Indian Policy Review Commission: AIPRC
Central Files: CF
Dwight D. Eisenhower Library: DDEL
Ewald Research Files: ERF
Fred Seaton Papers: FSP
General Files: GF
Glenn Emmons Papers: GEP
National Archives: NA
Official File: OF
Records of the Bureau of Indian Affairs: RBIA
Record Group: RG
South Dakota Oral History Center: SDOHC
University of New Mexico General Library: UNMGL
University of South Dakota: USD

## Chapter 1
## Introduction

1. Nancy Oestreich Lurie, "Historical Background," in *The American Indian Today,* ed. Stuart Levine and Nancy Oestreich Lurie, p. 69.

2. Wilcomb E. Washburn, *The Assault on Indian Tribalism: The General Allotment Law (Dawes Act) of 1887,* pp. 5–8, 18–22.

3. "General Allotment Act," in *The American Indian and the United States: A Documentary History,* vol. 3, ed. Wilcomb E. Washburn, pp. 2190–92.

4. Lurie, "Historical Background," p. 71; S. Lyman Tyler, *A History of Indian Policy,* p. 128; Theodore H. Haas, "The Legal Aspects of Indian Affairs from 1887 to 1957," p. 15.

5. Wilcomb E. Washburn, introduction to a reprint of the "Indian Citizenship Act," in Washburn, *The American Indian and the United States,* p. 2209.

6, Robert F. Berkhofer, Jr., *The White Man's Indian: Images of the American Indian from Columbus to the Present,* pp. 62–69, 180–81; Lewis Meriam, ed., *The Problems of Indian Administration,* passim.

7. "Wheeler-Howard Act," in Washburn, *The American Indian and the United States*, pp. 2210–17.

8. Larry J. Hasse, "Termination and Assimilation: Federal Indian Policy, 1943 to 1961," (Ph.D. diss., Washington State University, 1974), p. 34; J. Leiper Freeman, "Chapter Nine: The Bureau of Indian Affairs" (part of an administrative history of the Department of the Interior), n.d., p. 39, Box—BIA-Histories, Reports, AIPRC, RG 220, NA. For an example of the opposition to the IRA among older Indians who resented the dislocation of political arrangements on one reservation in South Dakota, Pine Ridge, see Joseph Cash interview with Jake Herman, Summer 1967, tape 38, SDOHC, USD; Graham D. Taylor, *The New Deal and American Indian Tribalism: The Administration of the Indian Reorganization Act, 1934–45*, contains an appraisal of the various divisions that hindered complete acceptance of the IRA.

9. Eric F. Goldman, *The Crucial Decade and After, 1945–1960*, p. 122. An example of the comparison of Indian communal social structure with international communism can be found in a speech before the Congress by Senator George Malone of Nevada in the *Congressional Record*, 83d Cong., 1st sess., 1953, 99, pp. 10294.

10. *Congressional Record*, 79th Cong., 1st sess., 1949, 98, Appendix: A4086; O. K. Armstrong, "Set the American Indian Free," *Reader's Digest*, August 1945, pp. 47–51.

11. Gerald D. Nash, *The American West in the Twentieth Century: A Short History of an Urban Oasis*, pp. 197–212. Statistics on the expansion of state and local government expenditure and the subsequent search for new revenue sources can be found in Glen E. Davies, "State Taxation on Indian Reservations," p. 132.

12. S. Lyman Tyler, *Indian Affairs: A Work Paper on Termination With an Attempt to Show Its Antecedents*, pp. 27, 29–30. A description of the anti-Collier congressional opposition appears in Hasse, "Termination and Assimilation," pp. 42–54.

13. Freeman, "Bureau of Indian Affairs," p. 42; Charles F. Wilkinson, "The Passage of the Termination Legislation," prepared for Task Force 10, pp. 16–17, Box—Taxation to Termination, AIPRC, RG 220, NA.

14. Tyler, *Indian Affairs*, p. 30; Nancy Oestreich Lurie, "The Indian Claims Commission Act," p. 58.

15. Tyler, *Indian Affairs*, pp. 29–33.

16. Hasse, "Termination and Assimilation," p. 94.

17. Freeman, "Bureau of Indian Affairs," pp. 25–27; Robert W. Young, *The Navajo Yearbook: 1951–1961, A Decade of Progress*, p. 1.

18. James E. Officer, "The American Indian and Federal Policy," in *The American Indian in Urban Society*, ed. Jack O. Waddell and O. Michael Watson, p. 47. An education specialist in the BIA at that time found a sense of rivalry between the education branch and the new relocation branch because of the widespread feeling among employees in the latter department that their task was to succeed where education had "failed." Madison Coombs to Larry Burt, 3/24/80, taped correspondence in author's files.

19. Hasse, "Termination and Assimilation," pp. 108–28; Patricia K. Ourada,

"Dillon Seymour Meyer, 1950–53," in *The Commissioners of Indian Affairs, 1824–1977,* ed. Robert M. Kvasnicka and Herman J. Viola, pp. 293–95.

20. Tyler, *Indian Affairs,* pp. 40–42.

# Chapter 2
# The Selection
# of an Indian Commissioner

1. Oliver La Farge, "Helping Elect the Great White Father," The *Santa Fe New Mexican,* October 28, 1952, clipping in Folder 11, Box I, GEP, UNMGL; U.S., Congress, Senate, *Nomination of Glenn L. Emmons: Hearings Before the Committee on Interior and Insular Affairs, United States Senate, Eighty-third Congress, First Session,* 1953, p. 90.

2. Oliver La Farge to Juan de Jesus Romero, Governor of Taos Pueblo, telegram, n.d., Box 310—Endorsements, GF, CF, DDEL.

3. La Farge, "Helping Elect the Great White Father," pp. 31, 33.

4. *American Banker,* August 7, 1952, n.p., and *Gallup Independent,* July 31, 1952, clippings in Folder 11, Box 1, GEP, UNMGL.

5. Jim Wright and Grace Edmister interview with Glenn Emmons, January 16, 1974, tape in Box V, GEP, UNMGL.

6. Ibid.

7. Ibid.

8. Ibid., *Gallup Independent,* July 31, 1952, and August 11, 1952, clippings in Folder 11, Box I, GEP, UNMGL.

9. *Gallup Independent,* December 12, 1952, clipping in Folder 7, Box II, GEP, UNMGL.

10. *Gallup Independent,* December 17, 1952, clipping in Folder 7, Box II, GEP, UNMGL.

11. Senate, *Nomination of Glenn L. Emmons,* p. 91; U.S., Congress, Senate, *Interior Department Appropriations for 1953: Hearings Before a Subcommittee of the Committee on Appropriations, United States Senate, Eighty-second Congress, Second Session, on H.R. 7176,* 1952, pp. 528–29, 861; La Farge, "Helping Elect the Great White Father," p. 33.

12. Debra R. Boender, "Glenn Emmons of Gallup," (M.A. thesis, University of New Mexico, 1976), pp. 61–62; Merle H. Tucker and Lee V. Langan to C. R. Megowen, December 16, 1952; W. E. Levis to Merle H. Tucker, December 22, 1952; W. E. Levis to Sidney J. Weinberg, December 22, 1952; Sidney J. Weinberg to W. E. Levis, December 24, 1952; and Laurence F. Lee to Charles F. Willis, Assistant to the President, January 21, 1953, Folder—Glenn Emmons, Box 310—Endorsements, GF, CF, DDEL.

13. Spokane meeting with Glenn Emmons, Minutes: Tribal Area Conferences, 1956, p. 13, Folder 13, Box III GEP, UNMGL; Jim Wright and Grace Edmister interview with Glenn Emmons; Cultural penetration accompanied the white advance into Navajo country. See Oren Arnold, "The Navajo Wind that Speaks," pp. 132–36.

14. The *Santa Fe New Mexican,* December 31, 1952, clipping in Folder—

Glenn Emmons, Box 310—Endorsements, GF, CF, DDEL; Jim Wright and Grace Edmister interview with Glenn Emmons.

15. *The New York Times*, January 11, 1953, p. 87; John Claw to Douglas McKay, January 1, 1953, Folder—Glenn Emmons, Box 310—Endorsements, GF, CF, DDEL.

16. *Christian Science Monitor*, February 7, 1953, p. 10, clipping in Folder 7, Box II, GEP, UNMGL; *The New York Times*, January 11, 1953, p. 87.

17. Theodore Bruelheids, Executive Secretary of Indian Council Fires, to Dwight D. Eisenhower, February 2, 1953, Folder—Commissioner of Indian Affairs, Box 310—Endorsements, GF, CF, DDEL; *The New York Times*, March 20, 1953, p. 15 and April 6, 1953, p. 24.

18. *Holdenville* (Oklahoma) *Daily News*, May 4, 1953, clipping in Folder—Belvin, Harry, Box 311—Endorsements, GF, CF, DDEL.

19. *The New York Times*, July 16, 1953, p. 22; Orme Lewis to Charles F. Willis, June 5, 1953, Folder—Commissioner of Indian Affairs, Box 310—Endorsements, GF, CF, DDEL; Senate, *Nomination of Glenn Emmons*, p. 93; Orme Lewis to Larry Burt, March 19, 1980, correspondence in author's files; Orme Lewis to Charles F. Willis, July 9, 1953, Folder 4-B—Bureau of Indian Affairs, 1953–1955, Box 117, OF, CF, DDEL; Jim Wright and Grace Edmister interview with Glenn Emmons.

20. Glenn Emmons to Larry Burt, January 18, 1974, correspondence in author's files; Boender, "Glenn Emmons," pp. 3–7.

21. Emmons to Burt, January 18, 1974; Boender, "Glenn Emmons," pp. 7, 14, 27–29.

22. Emmons to Burt, January 18, 1974; Boender, "Glenn Emmons," pp. 16, 34–36; Emmons for Governor Club, Press Release, May 16, 1944, Folder 1, Box I, GEP, UNMGL.

23. Jim Wright and Grace Edmister interview with Glenn Emmons; Emmons for Governor Club, Press Release, May 16, 1944.

24. José E. Armijo to Douglas McKay, May 7, 1953, Folder 3, Box II, GEP, UNMGL; *Carlsbad Current Argus*, July 16, 1953, clipping in Folder 7, Box II, GEP, UNMGL.

25. Will Harrison, "Federal Jobs for New Mexico Faithfuls Slow," *Santa Fe New Mexican*, March 10, 1953, clipping in Folder—Commissioner of Indian Affairs, Box 310—Endorsements, GF, CF, DDEL; "The Winners of No Election," *Time*, March 22, 1953, p. 29; *The New York Times*, July 9, 1953, p. 5.

26. Douglas McKay to Sherman Adams, July 9, 1953, and Orme Lewis to Charles F. Willis, July 9, 1953, Folder 4-B—Bureau of Indian Affairs, 1953–55, Box 117, OF, CF, DDEL.

27. Simpson did not fully cooperate with Mechem on the withdrawal matter. The White House released the statement to the press after Mechem informed Lewis that Simpson's withdrawal letter would be forthcoming. But shortly thereafter Simpson denied having removed himself from consideration. See *The New York Times*, July 16, 1953, p. 22, and Senate, *Nomination of Glenn Emmons*, pp. 62–63.

28. Senate, *Nomination of Glenn Emmons*, pp. 7–9; *Congressional Record*, 83d Cong., 1st Sess., 99, p. 9584.

29. *Congressional Record*, 83d Cong., 1st Sess., 99, pp. 8934–35, 9159.

30. *Arizona Republic*, July 17, 1953, clipping in Folder 7, Box II, GEP, UNMGL; *Congressional Record*, 83d Cong., 1st Sess., 99, p. 9583; *Anadarko Daily News*, July 17, 1953, n.p., clipping in Folder 7, Box II, GEP, UNMGL.

31. *Congressional Record*, 83d Cong., 1st Sess., 99, pp. 9172–73; George was probably referring to the Fernandez Company, a New Mexico livestock firm operated by Laurence's brother Floyd.

32. Ibid., pp. 9223–25, 9577–79, 9584; The *Santa Fe New Mexican*, July 22, 1953, clipping in Folder 7, Box II, GEP, UNMGL.

33. *Congressional Record*, 83d Cong., 1st Sess., 99, pp. 9583–84, 9718, 9720.

34. *Gallup Independent*, July 28, 1953, clipping in Folder 7, Box II, GEP, UNMGL.

35. Senate, *Nomination of Glenn Emmons*, pp. 50–52, 56, 59; *Congressional Record*, 83d Cong., 1st Sess., 99, p. 10275.

36. Laurence F. Lee to Glenn Emmons, August 6, 1953, Folder I, Box II, GEP, UNMGL; *Gallup Independent*, July 28, 1953, clipping in Folder 7, Box II, GEP, UNMGL.

## Chapter 3
## Formation of a Policy

1. Gary Orfield, "The Senator and the Indians," *A Study of the Termination Policy*, pp. 2–3.

2. Hans Kohn, *The Idea of Nationalism: A Study of Its Origin and Development* (New York, 1943), pp. 10–16, and Benjamin Schwartz, *In Search of Wealth and Power: Yen Fu and the West* (Cambridge, 1964), p. 19, both quoted in Boyd C. Shafer, *Nationalism: Its Nature and Interpreters*, pp. 8–9.

3. A succinct statement revealing conservative attitudes toward the sovereignty question made by Arthur V. Watkins, the Senate's leading proponent of federal withdrawal, can be found in U.S., Congress, *Termination of Federal Supervision Over Certain Tribes of Indians: Joint Hearings Before Subcommittees of the Committees on Interior and Insular Affairs, Eighty-third Congress, Second Session, on S. 2749 and H.R. 7322*, Part 5, 1954, p. 457.

4. Orme Lewis to Larry Burt, March 19, 1980, correspondence in author's files.

5. For an early expression of the "liberation" view of Indian policy by a former Republican representative from Missouri, see O. K. Armstrong, "Set the American Indian Free," *Reader's Digest*, August 1945, pp. 47–51. A similar analysis by Glenn Emmons over a decade later appears in an outline the commissioner made of a proposed book entitled *Freedom for the First Americans*, Folder 15, Box V, GEP, UNMGL.

6. For Watkins's view on the relationship between productivity and the right to occupy land see U.S., Congress, *Termination of Federal Supervision Over Certain Tribes of Indians: Joint Hearings Before Subcommittees of the Committees on Interior and Insular Affairs, Second Session, on S. 2750 and H.R. 7319*, Part 7, 1954, p. 936.

7. Angie Debo, *A History of the Indians of the United States*, pp. 121–22.

8. U.S., Congress, Senate, *Hearings Before a Subcommittee of the Committee on Appropriations: Interior Department Appropriations for 1954, United*

*States Senate, Eighty-third Congress, First Session, on H.R. 4828,* 1953, pp. 2, 18, 24.

9. U.S., Comptroller General of the United States, *Audit Report to the Congress of the United States, Bureau of Indian Affairs Department of the Interior, For the Fiscal Years Ended June 30, 1952 and 1953,* pp. 61, 89, Folder 4-B—Bureau of Indian Affairs, 1953–55, Box 117, OF, CF, DDEL; Walker River meeting with Glenn Emmons, Minutes: Tribal Area Conference, 1956, p. 27, Folder 3, Box III, GEP, UNMGL.

10. The credit figures can be found in U.S., Department of the Interior, Glenn Emmons, "Bureau of Indian Affairs," *Secretary of the Interior Annual Reports,* for the years 1953–60; Mohave-Chemehuevi meeting with Glenn Emmons, Minutes: Tribal Area Conferences, 1956, p. 260, Folder 9, Box III, GEP, UNMGL.

11. U.S., Department of the Interior, Glenn Emmons, "Bureau of Indian Affairs," *Secretary of the Interior Annual Reports,* 1954, p. 254; Cherokee meeting with Glenn Emmons, Minutes: Tribal Area Conferences, 1956, Folder 4, Box III, GEP, UNMGL.

12. Cherokee meeting with Emmons, pp. 3–6; Mohave-Chemehuevi meeting with Emmons, pp. 252–53.

13. Larry J. Hasse, "Termination and Assimilation: Federal Indian Policy, 1943 to 1961," (Ph.D. diss., Washington State University, 1974), p. 31. Nearly every congressional report on bills involving Indian affairs considered by the two Committees on Interior and Insular Affairs in 1953 included a summary of legislative goals in achieving withdrawal. For example, see U.S., Congress, House, *Amending Title 18, United States Code, Entitled "Crimes and Criminal Procedures," With Respect to State Jurisdiction Over Offenses Committed by or Against Indians in the Indian Country, and to Confer on the State of California Civil Jurisdiction Over Indians in the State,* H. Rept. 848 to Accompany H.R. 1063, 83d Cong., 1st Sess., 1953, pp. 3–5.

14. For a copy of House Concurrent Resolution 108 see U.S., Congress, House, *Information on Removal of Restrictions on American Indians: A Memorandum and Accompanying Information from the Chairman of the Committee on Interior and Insular Affairs, House of Representatives, to Members of the Committee,* Committee Print 38, 88th Cong., 2d Sess., 1964, p. 41; Orfield, "The Senator and the Indians," p. 2.

15. *The New York Times,* May 21, 1953, p. 33, and May 30, 1953, p. 17; U.S., Congress, House, *Transferring the Maintenance and Operation of Hospital and Health Facilities For Indians to the Public Health Service,* H. Rept. 870 To Accompany H.R. 303, 83d Cong., 1st Sess., 1953, pp. 10–11.

16. U.S., Congress, House, *Providing a Certificate or Decree of Competency for U.S. Indians in Certain Cases,* H. Rept. 836 To Accompany H.R. 4985, 83d Cong., 1st Sess., 1953, p. 7. Letters of opposition can be found in Folder 12, Box V, GEP, UNMGL; Comptroller General, *Audit Report for Fiscal Years 1952 and 1953,* p. 98.

17. *United States Statutes at Large,* 67, 83–277, pp. 586–87 and 83–281, p. 590.

18. U.S., Congress, Senate, *Background Report on Public Law 280,* Com-

mittee Print, 94th Cong., 1st Sess., 1975, pp. 3–5, found in Box—Preference, Indian, AIPRC, RG 220, NA.

19. Carole E. Goldberg, "Public Law 280: The Limits of State Jurisdiction Over Reservation Indians," p. 541; U.S., Congress, Senate, *Juvenile Delinquency (Indians): Hearings Before the Subcommittee to Investigate Juvenile Delinquency of the Committee on the Judiciary, United States Senate, Eighty-fourth Congress, First Session, Pursuant to S. Res. 62*, 1955, pp. 12–15.

20. Goldberg, "Public Law 280," p. 541; Senate, *Background Report on Public Law 280*, pp. 6, 12–16.

21. House, *Amending Title 18, United States Code*, p. 6; Hasse, "Termination and Assimilation," pp. 189–90.

22. D'Arcy McNickle, "U.S. Indian Speaks," p. 27; Goldberg, "Public Law 280," pp. 544–45; John Collier, "Indian Takeaway: Betrayal of a Trust," p. 290; *The New York Times*, August 8, 1953, p. 14.

23. Will Harrison, "Emmons Not Rushing Changes," The *Santa Fe New Mexican*, October 21, 1953, clipping in Folder 17, Box V, GEP, UNMGL; *The New York Times*, September 6, 1953, p. 38; Dwight D. Eisenhower to Glenn Emmons, September 2, 1953, quoted in "Address to be Delivered by Commissioner Glenn L. Emmons with Indian Tribal Groups during September, 1953," Folder 12, Box II, GEP, UNMGL *Minot* (North Dakota) *Daily News*, October 8, 1953, Muskogee (Oklahoma) *Daily Phoenix*, September 7, 1953, *Ponca City* (Oklahoma) *News*, September 13, 1953, and *Portland Oregonian*, October 11, 1953, clippings in Folder 17, Box V, GEP, UNMGL.

24. The phrase quoted belongs to Orme Lewis. The occasion was his appearance before an appropriations subcommittee. It can be found in U.S., Congress, House, *Interior Department Appropriations for 1955: Hearings Before the Subcommittee of the Committee on Appropriations, House of Representatives, Eighty-third Congress, Second Session*, 1954, p. 17; Glenn Emmons, "Future Prospects in Indian Affairs," address before the annual meeting of the Indian Rights Association, January 21, 1954, transcript in Folder 13, Box II, GEP, UNMGL.

25. Glenn Emmons, "Talk by Commissioner of Indian Affairs Glenn L. Emmons to Central Office Staff of the Bureau of Indian Affairs," December 21, 1953, p. 5, transcript in Folder 12, Box II, GEP, UNMGL; *The New York Times*, January 20, 1954, p. 14; Lewis to Burt, March 19, 1980.

26. A copy of the Bimson Report can be found in House Committee on Interior and Insular Affairs, *Survey Report of the Bureau of Indian Affairs*, Committee Print 14, January 26, 1954, Box—BIA-Histories Reports, AIPRC, RG 220, NA.

## Chapter 4
## The Drive to Terminate
## Various Tribes

1. The attendance records of subcommittee members at the joint hearings vividly illustrated the lack of attention given even to important legislation affecting Indians. In the Senate, only Watkins attended more than one of the thir-

teen sessions. House subcommittee chairman E. Y. Berry of South Dakota appeared regularly but allowed Watkins to dominate the questioning. Other members attended occasionally or not at all. In most cases only two or three congressmen joined their staff workers at the hearings; Gary Orfield, "The Senator and the Indians," *A Study of the Termination Policy*, p. 4.

2. U.S., Commission on Civil Rights, *Justice: 1961 United States Commission on Civil Rights*, Book 5, 1961, pp. 146–48.

3. A summary of the contents of termination bills appears in U.S., Congress, *Termination of Federal Supervision Over Certain Tribes of Indians: Joint Hearings Before Subcommittees of the Committees on Interior and Insular Affairs, Eighty-third Congress, Second Session, on S. 2670 and H.R. 7674*, 1954, pp. 42–43.

4. Heirship lands consisted of allotments jointly owned by more than one Indian. Under the Dawes Act the descendants of a deceased Indian inherited equal portions of the original allotment. By the 1950s hundreds of Native Americans sometimes held an interest in the same plot. BIA regulations required the consent of a majority of owners before heirship lands could be sold or partitioned. Since in many cases heirs could not be found, the land sat idle or was leased by non-Indians. The change in rules included in termination bills enabled the BIA to eliminate the heirship mess on a reservation prior to the termination date.

5. Congress, *Termination: Joint Hearings on S. 2670 and H.R. 7674*, pp. 42–43.

6. Ibid., pp. 44, 54–59, 60–62, 66, 82–83.

7. Ibid., p. 60; Oil and mineral leases on BIA-regulated Indian land tended to run for longer periods and paid approximately 4 percent less to native owners in royalties. See Marvin J. Sonosky, "Oil, Gas, and Other Minerals on Indian Reservation," pp. 232–33.

8. U.S., Congress, House, *Providing for Termination of Federal Supervision Over the Property of Certain Tribes, Bands, and Colonies of Indians in the State of Utah and the Individual Members Thereof*, VII, H. Rept. 2661 to Accompany S. 2670, 83d Cong., 2d Sess., 1954, p. 2; U.S., Congress, House, *Providing for the Termination of Federal Supervision Over the Property of Certain Tribes, Bands, and Colonies of Indians in the State of Utah and the Individual Members Thereof*, IV, H. Rept. 1904 to Accompany S. 2670, 83d Cong., 2d Sess., 1954, pp. 2–3; Congress, *Termination: Joint Hearings on S. 2670 and H.R. 7674*, pp. 62, 84.

9. The subsidization of public schools came under the authority of the 1934 Johnson-O'Malley Act, which allowed the secretary of the interior to contract with states for the education, medical care, agricultural assistance, or social welfare of Native Americans.

10. Sustained-yield refers to a type of scientific forest management in which harvests are regulated to ensure a continuing level of equal yearly cuts over the long term.

11. U.S., Congress, *Termination of Federal Supervision Over Certain Tribes of Indians: Joint Hearings Before Subcommittees of the Committees on Interior and Insular Affairs, Eighty-third Congress, Second-Session, on S. 2744, H.R. 6282, and H.R. 6547*, Part 2, 1954, pp. 99–104.

12. Ibid., pp. 99–100, 110–15; U.S., Congress, Senate, *Termination of Federal Supervision Over the Property of the Alabama-Coushatta Indians of Texas,* S. Rept. 1321 to Accompany S. 2744, 83d Cong., 2d Sess., 1954, p. 3.

13. U.S., Congress, *Termination of Federal Supervision Over Certain Tribes of Indians: Joint Hearings Before Subcommittees of the Committees on Interior and Insular Affairs, Eighty-third Congress, Second Session, on S. 2743 and H.R. 7318,* Part 11, 1954, pp. 1313, 1317, 1320–25, 1330, 1387–88.

14. U.S., Congress, AIPRC, *Report on Terminated and Nonfederally Recognized Indians,* 1976, pp. 33–36, 46–47.

15. U.S., Congress, House, *Providing for the Termination of Federal Supervision Over the Property of Certain Tribes and Bands of Indians Located in Western Oregon, and the Individual Members Thereof,* H. Rept. 2492 to Accompany S. 2746, 83d Cong., 2d Sess., 1954, p. 12; AIPRC, *Report on Terminated Indians,* pp. 44–45, 51.

16. House, *Providing for the Termination of Indians Located in Western Oregon,* p. 6; AIPRC, *Report on Terminated Indians,* p. 47.

17 .U.S., Congress, *Termination of Federal Supervision Over Certain Tribes of Indians: Joint Hearings Before Subcommittees of the Committees on Interior and Insular Affairs, Eighty-third Congress, Second Session, on S. 2745 and H.R. 7320,* Part 4, 1954, pp. 211–14.

18. AIPRC, *Report on Terminated Indians,* pp. 43–44; U.S., Congress, Senate, *Amendments to the Klamath Termination Act of 1954: Hearings Before the Subcommittee on Indian Affairs of the Committee on Interior and Insular Affairs, United States Senate, Eighty-fifth Congress, First Session, on S. 2047,* Part 1, 1957, pp. 157–58.

19. AIPRC; *Report on Terminated Indians,* pp. 45–46, 53–54; Larry J. Hasse, "Termination and Assimilation: Federal Indian Policy, 1943 to 1961," (Ph.D. diss., Washington State University, 1974), pp. 150–53; Orme Lewis to Larry Burt, March 19, 1980, correspondence in author's files.

20. AIPRC, *Report on Terminated Indians,* pp. 35–36; Hasse, "Termination and Assimilation," pp. 152–53, 221–22; U.S., Congress, House, *Providing for the Termination of Federal Supervision Over the Property of the Klamath Tribe of Indians and of the Individual Members Thereof,* H. Rept. 2483 to Accompany S. 2745, 83d Cong., 2d Sess., 1954, p. 6.

21. Hasse, "Termination and Assimilation," p. 223; Congress, *Termination: Joint Hearings on S. 2745 and H.R. 7320,* p. 22; U.S., Congress, *Termination of Federal Supervision Over Certain Tribes of Indians: Joint Hearings Before Subcommittees of the Committees on Interior and Insular Affairs, Eighty-third Congress, Second Session, on S. 2745 and H.R. 7320,* Part 4-A, 1954, pp. 25–26, 30, 74–76; U.S., Congress, Senate, *Termination of Federal Supervision Over the Property of the Klamath Tribe, Oregon,* S. Rept. 1631, 83d Cong., 2d Sess., 1954, p. 8.

22. Senate, *Termination of the Klamath Tribe,* p. 8; Senate, *Amendments to the Klamath Termination Act: Hearings,* pp. 242–43; Susan Hood, "Termination of the Klamath Indian Tribe of Oregon," pp. 382–83.

23. Ibid.; Senate, *Amendments to the Klamath Termination Act: Hearings,* pp. 242–43; Richard Neuberger, "How Oregon Rescued a Forest," p. 49.

24. U.S., Congress, *Termination of Federal Supervision Over Certain Tribes*

*of Indians: Joint Hearings Before Subcommittees of the Committees on Interior and Insular Affairs, Eighty-third Congress, Second Session, on H.R. 7981,* Part 9, 1954, pp. 1155–57, 1160–63, 1178; Hasse, "Termination and Assimilation," pp. 231–35.

25. U.S., Congress, *Termination of Federal Supervision Over Certain Tribes of Indians: Joint Hearings Before Subcommittees of the Committees on Interior and Insular Affairs, Eighty-third Congress, Second Session, on S. 2750 and H.R. 7319,* Part 7, 1954, pp. 779–80.

26. Larry Burt interview with Walter McDonald, July 20, 1980.

27. Congress, *Termination: Joint Hearings on S. 2750 and H.R. 7319,* pp. 866, 869–71, 956–59. Tribal Chairman Walter McDonald saw the split among the Indians as primarily between young and old, but since a higher percentage of those who had left homelands were young, the on-reservation versus off-reservation and young versus old evaluations of the factions that supported or opposed termination are similar and equally valid; Burt interview with McDonald, July 20, 1980.

28. Burt interview with McDonald, July 20, 1980.

29. Congress, *Termination: Joint Hearings on S. 2750 and H.R. 7319,* pp. 890–91, 904–5.

30. Ibid., pp. 791–93.

31. Ibid., pp. 789–90; Burt interview with McDonald, July 20, 1980.

32. Congress, *Termination: Joint Hearings on S. 2750 and H.R. 7319,* pp. 799–831; Burt interview with McDonald, July 20, 1980.

33. U.S., Congress, *Termination of Federal Supervision Over Certain Tribes of Indians: Joint Hearings Before Subcommittees of the Committees on Interior and Insular Affairs, Eighty-third Congress, Second Session, on S. 2747 and H.R. 7321,* Part 8, 1954, pp. 1030–34, 1040, 1045, 1047, 1068.

34. Ibid., pp. 1030–31, 1039, 1053, 1057, 1069–74.

35. Ibid., pp. 1030–32; "General History of Negotiations by Commissioner Glenn Emmons with the Everglades Miccosukee Indians of Florida, 1954–1960," pp. 1–8, Folder 6, Box V, GEP, UNMGL.

36. U.S., Congress, *Termination of Federal Supervision Over Certain Tribes of Indians: Joint Hearings Before Subcommittees of the Committees on Interior and Insular Affairs, Eighty-third Congress, Second Session, on S. 2748 and H.R. 7316,* Part 12, 1954, pp. 1424–26, 1463, 1493.

37. Ibid., pp. 1433, 1467, 1481, 1490–93, 1504.

38. U.S., Congress, *Termination of Federal Supervision Over Certain Tribes of Indians: Joint Hearings Before Subcommittees of the Committees on Interior and Insular Affairs, Eighty-third Congress, Second Session, on S. 2749 and H.R. 7322,* Part 5, 1954, pp. 370, 379, 496–98.

39. Ibid., pp. 496–98, 538–60.

40. Ibid., pp. 485–86, 490–98, 507–8, 512–14.

41. Ibid., pp. 375, 438–39. Two months after the joint hearings a field worker for the American Friends Service Committee conducted a series of interviews with California Indians to determine their opinions of termination and found them deeply split over the issue. See *The New York Times,* April 8, 1956, p. 48.

42. Congress, *Termination: Joint Hearings on S. 2749 and H.R. 7322,* pp. 469–74.

43. U.S., Congress, *Termination of Federal Supervision Over Certain Tribes*

*of Indians: Joint Hearings Before Subcommittees of the Committees on Interior and Insular Affairs, Eighty-third Congress, Second Session, on S. 2813, H.R. 2828, and H.R. 7135,* Part 6, 1954, pp. 589–90, 612–14.

44. Ibid., pp. 585–86; Nancy Oestreich Lurie, "Menominee Termination: From Reservation to Colony," pp. 260–61.

45. Congress, *Termination: Joint Hearings on S. 2813, H.R. 2828, and H.R. 7135,* pp. 595, 608–9, 715; Gary Orfield, "The Response of the Tribe," *A Study of the Termination Policy,* p. 5; Patricia K. Ourada, *The Menominee Indians: A History,* p. 191.

46. Orfield, "Response of the Tribe," p. 5; idem, "The Wisconsin Idea," *A Study of the Termination Policy,* p. 2.

47. Idem, "The Wisconsin Idea," p. 3; Congress, *Termination: Joint Hearings on S. 2813, H.R. 2828, and H.R. 7135,* pp. 587, 595.

48. Congress, *Termination: Joint Hearings on S. 2813, H.R. 2828, and H.R. 7135,* pp. 595–99, 650–55.

49. Gary Orfield, "The Menominees and the Congress," *A Study of the Termination Policy,* p. 5.

50. Glenn Emmons to Clifton Young, August 21, 1953, Folder 8, Box IV, GEP, UNMGL; U.S., Congress, *Termination of Federal Supervision Over Certain Tribes of Indians: Joint Hearings Before Subcommittees of the Committees on Interior and Insular Affairs, Eighty-third Congress, Second Session, on H.R. 7552,* Part 10, 1954, pp. 1212–13, 1222, 1230–31, 1235.

51. Congress, *Termination: Joint Hearings on H.R. 7552,* pp. 1221, 1224, 1230, 1235, 1240, 1242–43, 1245, 1248–49.

52. The *Minot Daily News* articles are reprinted in U.S., Congress, Senate, *Juvenile Delinquency (Indians): Hearings Before the Subcommittee to Investigate Juvenile Delinquency of the Committee of the Judiciary, Eighty-third Congress, Second Session, Pursuant to S. Res. 89,* 1954, pp. 225–41; Dorothy Bohn, " 'Liberating' the Indian: Euphemism for a Land Grab," p. 150; *The New York Times,* May 6, 1954, p. 35.

53. *The New York Times,* February 12, 1954, p. 9; *Congressional Record,* 83d Cong., 2d Sess., 100, Appendix, p. A5981.

54. U.S., Department of the Interior, Glenn Emmons, "Bureau of Indian Affairs," *Secretary of the Interior Annual Reports,* 1955, p. 232.

55. Ibid.; Interview Tape II, Uintah-Ouray Reservation, pp. 5–6, Uintah Interview, pp. 1–5, transcripts in Box—Termination: Interviews with Terminated Utes by Task Force 10, AIPRC, RG 220, NA; U.S., Congress, Senate, *Attorney Contracts with Indian Tribes,* S. Rept. 8, 83d Cong., 1st Sess., 1953, passim.

56. Arthur V. Watkins, "Termination of Federal Supervision: The Removal of Restrictions Over Indian Property and Person," p. 52; Klamath meeting with Glenn Emmons, Minutes: Tribal Area Conferences, 1956, p. 18, Folder 12, Box III, GEP, UNMGL.

## Chapter 5
## Withdrawal by Attrition

1. Glenn Emmons to Walter Kennedy, March 27, 1958, and Merle E. Selecman to Glenn Emmons, February 15, 1954, Folder 4, Box V, GEP, UNMGL.

2. Jim Wright and Grace Edmister interview with Glenn Emmons, January

16, 1974, tape in Box V, GEP, UNMGL. An example of Emmons's promotion of the "three-prong attack" can be found in the reprint of a speech delivered January 21, 1954, at the annual meeting of the Indian Rights Association in Glenn Emmons, "Future Prospects in Indian Affairs," pp. 4–5; The *Santa Fe New Mexican*, March 28, 1954, *New York Herald Tribune*, May 7, 1954, *Albuquerque Journal*, March 28, 1954, and *Washington Daily News*, July 1, 1954, clippings in Folder 18, Box V, GEP, UNMGL; "Point Four" refers to a proposed aid program that would distribute economic and technical assistance to undeveloped countries around the world.

3. Hopi meeting with Glenn Emmons, Minutes: Tribal Area Conferences, 1956, p. 85, Folder 9, Box III, GEP, UNMGL.

4. Glenn Emmons, "U.S. Aim: Give Indians a Chance," pp. 41–42, 51; Dean Rusk to Glenn Emmons, January 29, 1954, Folder 1, Box V, GEP, UNMGL.

5. The creation and early activities of the organization that later became the American Indian Development Fund are described in the first two years of correspondence in Folder 1, Box V, GEP, UNMGL; Glenn Emmons to Larry Burt, March 10, 1976, correspondence in author's files.

6. Robert W. Young, *The Navajo Yearbook: 1951–1961, A Decade of Progress*, pp. 14–16.

7. Ibid., pp. 16–18; the Emmons quote is found in Hopi meeting with Emmons, p. 64. For a description of the mobile trailer schools and their use in culturally assimilating Navajo children, sometimes over the objections of reluctant parents, see Joseph Stocker, "Trailer Teachers in Navajoland," pp. 26–29, and Minnio Gilliland, " 'Your Children Shall Learn Paper': A Report on Navajo Education," pp. 558–60; Madison Coombs to Larry Burt, March 24, 1980, tape in author's files.

8. Young, *Navajo Yearbook*, pp. 33, 39.

9. Margaret Connell Szasz, *Education and the American Indian: The Road to Self-Determination Since 1928*, pp. 65–66, 123–24.

10. U.S., Congress, House, *The Supplemental Appropriation Bill, 1955: Hearings Before Subcommittees of the Committee on Appropriations, House of Representatives, Eighty-third Congress, Second Session*, Part 2, 1954, pp. 279–80, 1082, 1093; U.S., Congress, House, *Supplemental Appropriation Bill, 1955*, H. Rept. 2663 to Accompany H.R. 9936, 83d Cong., 2d Sess., p. 14; *Congressional Record*, 83d Cong., 2d Sess., 100, pp. 7702–6; Wright and Edmister interview with Emmons, January 16, 1974.

11. U.S., Department of the Interior, Glenn Emmons, "Bureau of Indian Affairs," *Secretary of the Interior Annual Reports*, 1954, pp. 235–36; *Congressional Record*, 83d Cong., 2d Sess., 100, p. 12298; Orme Lewis to Larry Burt, March 19, 1980, correspondence in author's files; *The New York Times*, August 15, 1954, p. 70.

12. U.S., Congress, House, *Transferring the Maintenance and Operation of Hospital and Health Facilities For Indians to the Public Health Service*, H. Rept. 870 to Accompany H.R. 303, 83d Cong., 1st Sess., 1953, p. 6.

13. U.S., Congress, Senate, *Transferring the Maintenance and Operation of Hospital and Health Facilities for Indians to the Public Health Service*, S. Rept. 1530, 83d Cong., 2d Sess., 1954, pp. 6–11; *Congressional Record*, 83d Cong., 2d Sess., 100, p. 11023.

14. Senate, *Transferring Health Facilities to the Public Health Service*, pp. 16–19; *The New York Times*, December 18, 1955, p. 76; Wright and Edmister interview with Emmons, January 16, 1974. For statistics on the improvement in Indian health after 1955 see Alan L. Sorkin, *American Indians and Federal Aid*, pp. 51–54. Expressions of Indian discontent with the distances to PHS hospitals in some cases can be found in oral history collections, such as Vince Pratt interview with George and Chuck Allen, Summer, 1971, tape 827, SDOHC, USD, and in numerous places throughout the transcripts of the 1956 Commissioner's Conferences in Folders 1–14, Minutes: Tribal Area Conferences, 1956, Box III, GEP, UNMGL.

15. U.S., Congress, *Agricultural Extension Work Among Indians, Transfer to the Department of Agriculture: Joint Hearings Before Subcommittees of the Committees on Interior and Insular Affairs, Eighty-third Congress, Second Session, on S. 3385 and H.R. 8982*, 1954, pp. 3–5.

16. Ibid., pp. 5–8, 13–17, 22; *Congressional Record*, 83d Cong., 2d Sess., 100, pp. 8976, 14283.

17. *Congressional Record*, 83d Cong., 2d Sess., 100, Appendix, p. A5650; Arthur V. Watkins to Bernard M. Shanley, Counsel for the President, July 9, 1954, Folder 121 (1)—Indians, Box 618, OF, CF, DDEL; U.S., Congress, Senate, *Amending the Act Entitled "To Confer Jurisdiction on the States of California, Minnesota, Nebraska, Oregon, and Wisconsin, With Respect to Criminal Offenses and Civil Causes of Action Committed or Arising on Indian Reservations Within Such States," S. Rept. 357 to Accompany S. 51, 84th Cong., 1st Sess.*, 1955, pp. 1–2.

18. Glenn Emmons Memorandum to All Area Directors and Superintendents, Washington Division, and Branch Heads, January 19, 1954, Folder 9, Box IV, GEP, UNMGL; U.S., Congress, Senate, *Interior Department Appropriations for 1955: Hearings Before a Subcommittee on Appropriations, United States Senate, Eighty-third Congress, Second Session, on H.R. 8680*, 1954, p. 747; U.S., Department of the Interior, Glenn Emmons, "Bureau of Indian Affairs," *Secretary of the Interior Annual Reports*, 1956, p. 214.

19. "The Bureau of Indian Affairs Voluntary Relocation Program," found in BIA to Sarah McClendon, March 16, 1959, p. 3, Folder 14, Box IV, GEP, UNMGL; LaVerne Madigan, *The American Indian Relocation Program*, pp. 10–12; Dennis Carroll, "Relocation and the Urban Indian," pp. 11–13, Box—Urban and Rural Indians, AIPRC, RG 220, NA; U.S., Comptroller General of the United States, *Report to the Congress of the United States: Administration of Withdrawal Activities by the Bureau of Indian Affairs, Department of the Interior*, 1958, pp. 20–24, Folder 4-B(2)—Bureau of Indian Affairs, 1956-1960, Box 117, OF, CF, DDEL. For firsthand descriptions of housing and neighborhoods see Cynthia Kelsey interview with Naomi Warren La Due, August 14, 1968, tape 224 and anonymous interview by Joseph Cash (restricted use), August 25, 1967, tape, SDOHC, USD.

20. Madigan, *Indian Relocation Program*, pp. 10–11; *The New York Times*, December 16, 1956, p. 75; Carroll, "Relocation and the Urban Indian," p. 29.

21. Herbert Hoover interview with Alfred DuBray, July 28, 1970, tape 533, SDOHC, USD.

22. Carroll, "Relocation and the Urban Indian," p. 28; Joan Ablon, "Ameri-

146 NOTES

can Indian Relocation: Problems of Dependency and Management in the City,"
p. 363; General Session, Oklahoma, Kansas, Mississippi Conference, Minutes:
Tribal Area Conferences, 1956, Folder 8, Box III, GEP, UNMGL.

23. Donald L. Fixico, "Termination and Relocation: Federal Indian Policy in
the 1950s," (Ph.D. diss., University of Oklahoma, 1980), pp. 230–31; Vince Pratt
interview with Oliver D. Eastman, August 3, 1971, tape 768, SDOHC, USD; Alan
Sorkin interview with BIA Employment Assistance Officer, July, 1968, quoted
in Sorkin, Indians and Federal Aid, p. 121.

24. Comptroller General, Report to the Congress: Withdrawal Activities, pp.
24–25; Gerald Wolff interview with Lenora DeWitt, August 25, 1971, tape 786
and Pratt interview with Eastman, SDOHC, USD.

25. Willard Fraser interview with Eloise Pease, September 10, 1970, tape 599
and Herbert Hoover interview with Gordon Jones, June 2, 1971, tape 684,
SDOHC, USD.

26. U.S., Department of the Interior, Barton Greenwood, "Bureau of Indian
Affairs," Secretary of the Interior Annual Reports, 1953, pp. 50–51; U.S., Department of the Interior, Glenn Emmons, "Bureau of Indian Affairs," Secretary
of the Interior Annual Reports, 1960, p. 225.

27. Clyde W. Pensoneau, "New Contracts: Legislative or Executive Order,"
p. 1, and James F. Canan, "Accomplishments to Date in Extension Contracts
in Colorado," p. 1, both delivered before the Tri-Area Resources Conference in
Phoenix, Arizona, January 27–29, 1958, transcripts in Box 369 (68A–2045, 14/46:
48–5), RBIA, RG 75, NA. The last citation reflects the numbering system used by
the BIA. Since the documents are so recent, they still belong to the BIA and are
located in the National Records Center in Suitland, Maryland. At some future
date they will be deposited in the National Archives and catalogued in the Record Group shown.

28. For examples to illustrate this dilemma, see Joseph Cash interview with
Julis and Jack Rustemeyer, Summer, 1967, tape 39, Joseph Cash interview with
Louis Leader Charge, Summer, 1968, tape 76, and Joseph Cash interview with
Floyd E. Taylor, August 9, 1968, tape 50, SDOHC, USD.

29. Pine Ridge meeting with Glenn Emmons, Minutes: Tribal Area Conferences, 1956, p. 2, Box 369 (68A–2045, 14/46: 48-5), RBIA, RG 75, NA; Address by
Glenn Emmons before the twelfth annual convention of the National Congress
of American Indians, 1955, p. 2, transcript in Folder 14, Box II, GEP, UNMGL.

30. Greenwood, "Bureau of Indian Affairs," 1953, p. 32; Emmons, "Bureau
of Indian Affairs," 1954, p. 245; Larry J. Hasse, "Termination and Assimilation:
Federal Indian Policy, 1943 to 1961" (Ph.D. diss., Washington State University,
1974), p. 247; U.S., Congress, House, Department of the Interior and Related
Agencies Appropriations for 1961: Hearings Before a Subcommittee of the
Committee on Appropriations, House of Representatives, Eighty-sixth Congress, Second Session, Part 1, 1960, pp. 637–38; Glenn Emmons to Files, Memorandum, May 16, 1955, Folder 10, Box IV, GEP, UNMGL; Address by Emmons
before NCAI, p. 4; Walker River meeting with Glenn Emmons, Minutes: Tribal
Area Conferences, 1956, pp. 29–30, Folder 3, Box III, GEP, UNMGL.

31. Comptroller General, Report to the Congress: Withdrawal Activities, p. 15.

32. U.S., Congress, House, Authorizing the Leasing of Restricted Indian

*Lands for Public, Religious, Educational, Recreational, Residential, Business, and Other Purposes Requiring the Grant of Long-Term Leases,* H. Rept. 1562 to Accompany S. 34, 84 Cong., 1 Sess., 1955, p. 3; Wright and Edmister interview with Emmons, January 16, 1974; Reid Peyton Chambers and Monroe E. Price, "Discretion and the Leasing of Indian Lands," pp. 1063–64.

33. Emmons, "Bureau of Indian Affairs," 1954, p. 258; Emmons, "Bureau of Indian Affairs," 1955, p. 263; Coombs to Burt, March 24, 1980.

34. *The New York Times,* January 22, 1955, p. 6; *Washington Post and Times Herald,* January 9, 1956, reprinted in *Congressional Record,* 84 Cong., 2 Sess., 102, p. 3805.

35. U.S., Congress, Senate, *Juvenile Delinquency (Indians): Hearings Before the Subcommittee to Investigate Juvenile Delinquency of the Committee on the Judiciary, United States Senate, Eighty-fourth Congress, First Section, Pursuant to S. Res. 62,* 1955, pp. 67–68; General Conference with Washington and Oregon Tribes, Minutes: Tribal Area Conferences, 1956, p. 14, Folder 12, Box III, GEP, UNMGL U.S., Congress, House, *Alaska Native Loan Program: Twenty-fifth Report by the Committee on Government Operations,* Rept. 1821, 85 Cong., 2 Sess., 1958, pp. 3, 7–10.

36. *Congressional Record,* 85 Cong., 1 Sess., 103, Appendix, p. A6949–50.

37. U.S., Congress, Senate, *Klamath Indian Tribe—Termination of Federal Supervision: Hearings Before the Committee on Interior and Insular Affairs and Its Subcommittee on Indian Affairs, United States Senate, Eighty-fourth Congress, Second Session,* 1956, p. 8; *Congressional Record,* 84th Cong., 2d Sess., 102, pp. 5446–50.

38. *The New York Times,* July 10, 1955, p. 64; U.S., Congress, Senate, Amendments to the Klamath Termination Act of 1954: Hearings Before the Subcommittee on Indian Affairs of the Committee on Interior and Insular Affairs, United States Senate, Eighty-fifth Congress, First Session, on S. 2047, Part 1, 1957, pp. 50–51.

39. Senate, *Amendments to the Klamath Termination Act,* pp. 284–87; U.S., Congress, Senate, *Interior Department and Related Agencies Appropriations for 1957: Hearings Before a Subcommittee of the Committee on Appropriations, United States Senate, Eighty-fourth Congress, Second Session, on H.R. 9390,* 1956, pp. 802–803, 811.

40. Gary Orfield, "The Response of the Tribe," *A Study of the Termination Policy,* pp. 9–11; idem., "The Shuffling of the Papers," Ibid., pp. 10–11.

41. Orfield, "The Response of the Tribe," pp. 8, 11.

# Chapter 6
## Opposition Intensifies

1. The relationship between the way the BIA carried out termination bills and the escalating opposition can be seen in the appearance by George M. Keith, Wisconsin Deputy Director of the Department of Public Welfare, before the 1955 annual meeting of the Governors' Interstate Indian Council. He described to officials from other states the difficulties of working out a program in the

little time before the deadline. The council that only a few years earlier had called for federal withdrawal from Indian affairs then passed resolutions demanding that Washington consider its responsibility more carefully in Indian health, education, welfare, and economic opportunity. See *The New York Times*, October 7, 1955, p. 26, and S. Lyman Tyler, *Indian Affairs: A Work Paper on Termination With an Attempt to Show Its Antecedents*, p. 51.

2. U.S., Congress, House, *Interior Department and Related Agencies Appropriations for 1956: Hearings Before the Subcommittee of the Committee on Appropriations, House of Representatives, Eighty-fourth Congress, First Session*, 1955, p. 212; *The New York Times*, January 24, 1955, p. 23; Tyler, *Indian Affairs*, p. 50.

3. Tyler, *Indian Affairs*, p. 42; House, *Appropriations for 1956: Hearings*, p. 212; *The New York Times*, March 28, 1955, p. 21.

4. House, *Appropriations for 1956: Hearings*, p. 212; *Congressional Record*, 84th Cong., 1st Sess., 101, pp. 11954–55.

5. *The New York Times*, June 27, 1955, p. 21.

6. *The New York Times*, September 11, 1955, p. 126; Harold E. Fey, "What Indians Want," p. 1080.

7. Douglas McKay to Oliver La Farge, November 30, 1955, Folder 6, Box V, GEP, UNMGL.

8. Harold E. Fey, "Record Interest in American Indians," p. 637; *The New York Times*, May 19, 1955, p. 16.

9. Useful examples of articles written by Harold Fey at this time include "Navajo Race With Tragedy" and "Indian Winter."

10. U.S., Congress, Senate, *Interior Department and Related Agencies Appropriations for 1956: Hearings Before a Subcommittee of the Committee on Appropriations, United States Senate, Eighty-fourth Congress, First Session, on H.R. 5085*, 1955, pp. 402, 424–25.

11. Ibid., pp. 402, 404. State officials seemed just as concerned over their inability to control the "sexual immorality" that led to cases of nonsupport among unwed Indian mothers as they were over possible overpayment resulting from the lack of authority to search out fathers; Glenn Emmons, "Federal-State Relations in Indian Affairs," transcript of October 1, 1954, address before the Governors' Interstate Indian Council, found in Folder 13, Box II, GEP, UNMGL.

12. Senate, *Interior Department Appropriations for 1956: Hearings*, pp. 403–6.

13. U.S., Congress, Senate, *Juvenile Delinquency (Indians): Hearings Before the Subcommittee to Investigate Juvenile Delinquency of the Committee on the Judiciary, United States Senate, Eighty-third Congress, Second Session, Pursuant to S. Res, 89*, 1954, pp. 1–3.

14. Ibid., passim; U.S., Congress, Senate, *Juvenile Delinquency (Indians): Hearings Before the Subcommittee to Investigate Juvenile Delinquency of the Committee on the Judiciary, United States Senate, Eighty-fourth Congress, First Session, Pursuant to S. Res. 62*, 1955, pp. 94–135.

15. Senate, *Juvenile Delinquency (Indians): Hearings, Pursuant to S. Res. 62*, pp. 40–43.

16. Ibid., pp. 159–61; Senate, *Juvenile Delinquency (Indians): Hearings, Pursuant to S. Res. 89*, pp. 120–29.

17. Senate, *Juvenile Delinquency (Indians): Hearings, Pursuant to S. Res.*

89, pp. 120–29, 146–48. Additional testimony about the inadequacies of both the cattle loan program and RFC can be found in Gerald Wolff interview with Clyde Gildersleeve, August 23, 1972, tape 876; Joyce Aschenbrenner interview with Fred Jones, July 29, 1968, tape 155; and anonymous interview by Joseph Cash (restricted use), August 25, 1967, tape 18, SDOHC, USD.

18. U.S., Congress, Senate, *Juvenile Delinquency Among the Indians: Report of the Committee on the Judiciary, United States Senate, Made by Its Subcommittee to Investigate Juvenile Delinquency Pursuant to S. Res. 62 as Extended*, S. Rept. 1483, 84 Cong., 2 Sess., 1956, pp. 3–7, 16–51; *The New York Times*, September 11, 1955, p. 125.

19. U.S., Congress, House, *Interior Department and Related Agencies Appropriations for 1956: Hearings Before the Subcommittee of the Committee on Appropriations, United States House of Representatives, Eighty-fourth Congress, First Session*, 1955, p. 214; David T. Beals to Clyde Kluckhohn, December 9, 1954; David T. Beals to Roswell Magill, January 10, 1955; William B. Given to David T. Beals, April 18, 1955; Glenn L. Emmons to Mrs. C. V. Whitney, June 23, 1955; Lloyd D. Reynolds to Glenn L. Emmons, February 28, 1955; Jane E. Hinchcliffe to Glenn L. Emmons, December 26, 1956; and Glenn L. Emmons to David T. Beals, December 31, 1956, all found in Folder 1, Box V, GEP, UNMGL.

20. Charles Cooper, "New Hope," pp. 24–26, 51; Jicarilla meeting with Glenn Emmons, Minutes: Tribal Area Conferences, 1956, pp. 11–12, Folder 5, Box III, GEP, UNMGL.

21. Glenn Emmons, "Industry Moves to Indian Country," *Industrial Development* (June 1956), inserted by Republican Senator Barry Goldwater into the *Congressional Record*, 85th Cong., 1st Sess., 103, Appendix, p. A5777; U.S., Congress, House, *Department of the Interior and Related Agencies Appropriations for 1957: Hearings Before the Subcommittee of the Committee on Appropriations, United States House of Representatives, Eighty-fourth Congress, Second Session*, 1956, p. 443.

22. Robert A. White, "American Indian Crisis," pp. 207–8; Alan L. Sorkin, "American Indians Industrialize to Combat Poverty," p. 22.

23. U.S., Congress, Senate, *Federal Indian Policy: Hearings Before the Subcommittee of the Committee on Interior and Insular Affairs, United States Senate, Eighty-fifth Congress, First Session, on S. 809, S. Con. Res. 3, and S. 331*, 1957, pp. 255–57; Fort Berthold meeting with Glenn Emmons, Minutes: Tribal Area Conferences, 1956, p. 24, Folder 1, Box III, GEP, UNMGL; Sorkin, "American Indians Industrialize," p. 23.

24. Sisseton meeting with Glenn Emmons, Minutes: Tribal Area Conferences, 1956, pp. 13–15, Folder 2, Box III, GEP, UNMGL.

25. U.S., Department of the Interior, Glenn Emmons, "Bureau of Indian Affairs," *Secretary of the Interior Annual Reports*, 1957, p. 240; U.S., Congress, House, *Department of the Interior and Related Agencies Appropriations for 1961: Hearings Before a Subcommittee of the Committee on Appropriations, United States House of Representatives, Eighty-sixth Congress, Second Session*, Part 1, 1960, p. 639.

26. Emmons, "Industry Moves to Indian Country," p. A5777; Fort Berthold meeting with Emmons, p. 24.

' 27. Madison Coombs to Larry Burt, March 24, 1980, tape in author's files; Glenn Emmons, transcript of an address delivered before an Industrial Development Workshop at the University of Arizona, March 8, 1958, Folder 15, Box II, GEP, UNMGL.

28. U.S., Congress, Senate, *Second Supplemental Appropriation Bill, 1956: Hearings Before the Committee on Appropriations, United States Senate, Eighty-fourth Congress, Second Session, on H.R. 10004,* 1956, p. 299; U.S., Congress, Senate, *Interior Department and Related Agencies Appropriations for 1957: Hearings Before a Subcommittee of the Committee on Appropriations, United States Senate, Eighty-fourth Congress, Second Session, on H.R. 9390,* 1956, pp. 172–74; *Congressional Record,* 84 Cong., 2 Sess., 102, pp. 1521–22; U.S., Congress, House, *Directing the Secretary of the Interior to Conduct a Study and Investigation of Indian Education in the United States,* H. Rept. 2381 to Accompany H.J. Res. 451, 84 Cong., 2 Sess., 1956, pp. 1–2; U.S., Congress, House, *Second Supplemental Appropriation Bill, 1956,* H. Rept. 1897 to Accompany H.R. 10004, 84 Cong., 2 Sess., 1956, p. 22.

29. *Congressional Record,* 84th Cong., 1st Sess., 101 p. 11454, and 84th Cong., 2d Sess., 102, pp. 2986–87.

30. *Congressional Record,* 84th Cong., 2d Sess., 102, p. 379–80.

31. Ruth Mulvey Harmer, "Uprooting the Indian," *Atlantic Monthly,* March 1956; Dorothy Van De Mark, "The Raid on the Reservations," *Harper's Magazine,* March 1956; "Repartee," *Atlantic Monthly,* June 1956, pp. 20–23; "Letters," *Harper's Magazine,* May 1956, pp. 4, 6, 8, 10.

32. U.S., Department of the Interior, Glenn Emmons, "Bureau of Indian Affairs," *Secretary of the Interior Annual Reports,* 1956, p. 231; Department of the Interior Information Service, "Voluntary Relocation Program of Indian Bureau to Be Greatly Enlarged," Press Release for June 27, 1956, pp. 1–2, Folder—Indians (1), Box 12, FSP, ERF, DDEL.

33. U.S., Congress, House, *Providing Vocational Training for Adult Indians,* H. Rept. 2532 to Accompany H.R. 9904, 84th Cong., 2d Sess., 1956, pp. 1–2; U.S., Congress, Senate, *Relative to Employment for Certain Adult Indians On or Near Indian Reservations,* S. Rept. 2264 to Accompany S. 3416, 84th Cong., 2d Sess., 1956, pp. 2–3; Dennis Carroll, "Relocation and the Urban Indian," pp. 18–21, Box—Urban and Rural Indians, AIPRC, RG 220, NA.

34. Carroll, "Relocation and the Urban Indian," p. 19; Emmons, "Industry Moves to Indian Country," p. A5777; Sorkin, "American Indians Industrialize," pp. 20, 23.

35. *The New York Times,* October 6, 1955, p. 18; Glenn Emmons to Area Directors and Superintendents, April 12, 1956, pp. 1–6, Folder—Indians (2), Box 12, FSP, ERF, DDEL.

36. U.S., Department of the Interior, Glenn Emmons, "Bureau of Indian Affairs," *Secretary of the Interior Annual Reports,* 1957, p. 241; Aubrey Graves, "Today's Powwows Aren't Just Talk," *Washington Post and Times Herald,* n.d., inserted by Montana Democratic Representative Lee Metcalf into the *Congressional Record,* 85th Cong., 1st Sess., 103, Appendix, p. A783; Jim Wright and Grace Edmister interview with Glenn Emmons, January 16, 1974, tape in Box V, GEP, UNMGL.

37. Hopi meeting with Glenn Emmons, Folder 9, p. 64; Rocky Boy's meeting with Glenn Emmons, Folder 10, pp. 8–9; and All-Pueblo meeting with Glenn Emmons, Folder 5, p. 2, Minutes: Tribal Area Conferences, 1956, Box III, GEP, UNMGL.

38. Hopi meeting with Emmons, p. 65–67; Rocky Boy's meeting with Emmons, pp. 9–10.

39. Navajo meeting with Glenn Emmons, Folder 5, p. 2, and Havasupai meeting with Glenn Emmons, Folder 9, p. 195, Minutes: Tribal Area Conferences, 1956, Box III, GEP, UNMGL; Father Eugene Botelho, "Letters to the Editor," *Arizona Highways*, November 1957, p. 36. Although Native American attitudes toward public schools were clearly split, Indian oral history collections are replete with objections to them, especially the distances from reservations, the inevitable assimilation of non-Indian culture, and the social trauma for children who lack the money, clothing, and status enjoyed by most white youngsters. See Gerald Wolff interview with Madline Eagle Thunder, September 2, 1971, tape 801, and Joseph Cash interview with Purcell Rainwater, Summer 1967, tape 34, SDOHC, USD.

40. Group Reports, Aberdeen Area Conference, Minutes: Tribal Area Conferences, 1956, p. 42, Folder 2, Box III, GEP, UNMGL; "Position Paper of the National Convention for the Amendment of Public Law 83–280," pp. 2–3; National American Indian Court Judges Association, *Justice and the American Indian, Volume 1: The Impact of Public Law 280 upon the Administration of Criminal Justice on Indian Reservations*, p. 36; and "Demography of the State of Nevada," p. 10, all found in Box—Preference, Indian, AIPRC, RG 220, NA; Emmons, "Bureau of Indian Affairs," 1957, p. 253.

41. Omaha meeting with Glenn Emmons, Minutes: Tribal Area Conferences, 1956, pp. 2–4, Folder 1, Box III, GEP, UNMGL.

42. Turtle Mountain meeting with Glenn Emmons, Folder 1, p. 7, and Flathead meeting with Glenn Emmons, Folder 10, p. 1, Minutes: Tribal Area Conferences, 1956, Box III, GEP, UNMGL.

43. Final Session, Billings Area Conference, Folder 10, p. 5, and Pine Ridge meeting with Glenn Emmons, Folder 2, pp. 20–21, Minutes: Tribal Area Conferences, 1956, Box III, GEP, UNMGL.

44. Taos Pueblo meeting with Glenn Emmons, Folder 5, p. 13; Jemez Pueblo meeting with Glenn Emmons, Folder 5, pp. 6–7; and Winnebago meeting with Glenn Emmons, Folder 1, pp. 3–4, Minutes: Tribal Area Conferences, 1956, Box III, GEP, UNMGL.

45. Nambe Pueblo and Tesuque Pueblo meeting with Glenn Emmons, Folder 5, p. 17, Rosebud meeting with Glenn Emmons, Folder 2, p. 3, Question and Discussion Period, First Aberdeen Area Session, Folder 1, pp. 23–25, and Yavapai Apache meeting with Glenn Emmons, Folder 9, pp. 141–42, Minutes: Tribal Area Conferences, 1956, Box III, GEP, UNMGL.

46. McDermitt meeting with Glenn Emmons, Minutes: Tribal Area Conferences, 1956, pp. 70–79, Folder 3, Box III, GEP, UNMGL.

47. Warm Springs meeting with Glenn Emmons, Minutes: Tribal Area Conferences, 1956, pp. 20–21, Folder 12, Box III, GEP, UNMGL.

48. Graves, "Today's Powwows Aren't Just Talk," p. A783–84.

49. Ibid.; General Session, Portland Area Conference, Folder 13, p. 37, and Group Discussion, Billings Area Conference, Folder 10, pp. 9–10, Minutes: Tribal Area Conferences, 1956, Box III, GEP, UNMGL. Another participant at the Salt Lake City conference, Flathead Tribal Chairman Walter McDonald, confirmed Iliff McKay's impressions concerning BIA efforts to gain endorsements of unpopular policies. Larry Burt interview with Walter McDonald, July 20, 1980.

50. Graves, "Today's Powwows Aren't Just Talk," pp. A783–84; *El Paso Times*, August 26, 1956, *Denver Post*, August 21, 1956, and *Portland Oregonian*, September 16, 1956, clippings in Folder 19, Box V, GEP, UNMGL.

51. U.S., Congress, House, *Department of the Interior and Related Agencies Appropriations for 1958: Hearings Before a Subcommittee of the Committee on Appropriations, United States House of Representatives, Eighty-fifth Congress, First Session*, 1957, pp. 381–82; Emmons, "Bureau of Indian Affairs," 1957, p. 245; Lee Metcalf, "The Need For Revision of Federal Policy in Indian Affairs," p. 3.

52. U.S., Congress, House, *Providing for the Termination of Federal Supervision Over the Property of the Wyandotte Tribe of Oklahoma and the Individual Members Thereof*, H. Rept. 2804 to Accompany S. 3970, 84th Cong., 2d Sess., 1956, pp. 1–6; U.S., Congress, House, *Providing for the Termination of Federal Supervision Over the Property of the Peoria Tribe of Indians in the State of Oklahoma and the Individual Members Thereof*, H. Rept. 2802 to Accompany S. 3968, 84th Cong., 2d Sess., 1956, pp. 1–5; U.S., Congress, House, *Providing for the Termination of Federal Supervision Over the Property of the Ottawa Tribe of Indians in Oklahoma and the Individual Members Thereof*, H. Rept. 2803 to Accompany S. 3969, 84th Cong., 2d Sess., 1956, pp. 1–6; Emmons, "Bureau of Indian Affairs," 1957, pp. 242–43.

53. Joseph Cash interview with Walter Gene Jennison, June 3, 1976, tape 1022, and Joseph Cash interview with Charles E. Dawes, June 5, 1976, tape 1019, SDOHC, USD.

54. Homer M. Gilliand, "Soil and Moisture Conservation Topic: Termination, Policy, and Plans—At What Point Should Termination be Accomplished?" delivered before the Tri-Area Resources Conference in Phoenix, Arizona, January 27–29, 1958, pp. 1–2, transcript in Box 369 (68A–2045, 14/46: 48–5), RBIA, RG 75, NA.

55. Wilson C. Gutzman, "Problems and Obligations Related to Assumption of Range Management Responsibilities by Indians," delivered before the Tri-Area Resources Conference in Phoenix, Arizona, January 27–29, 1958, pp. 12–13, transcript in Box 369 (68A–2045, 14/46: 48–5), RBIA, RG 75, NA.

56. William L. Schroeder, "Operation and Maintenance of Range Improvement by Indians," delivered before the Tri-Area Resources Conference in Phoenix, Arizona, January 27–29, 1958, pp. 3–4, transcript in Box 369 (68A–2045, 14/46: 48–5), RBIA, RG 75, NA; U.S., Department of the Interior, Glenn Emmons, "Bureau of Indian Affairs," *Secretary of the Interior Annual Reports*, 1959, p. 264.

57. Barton O. Wetzel, "Education and Training of Indians in Preparation of Withdrawal," p. 2; Reino R. Sarlin, "Accomplishments to Date Leading to Withdrawal in the Gallup Area," p. 2; and Harry R. Kallander, "Accomplishments

to Date Leading to Withdrawal in the Phoenix Area," p. 2, all delivered before the Tri-Area Resources Conference in Phoenix, Arizona, January 27–29, 1958, transcripts in Box 369 (68A–2045, 14/46: 48–5), RBIA, RG 75, NA.

## Chapter 7
## Growing Battle
## Over Development

1. "Broken Arrow," *Time*, March 4, 1957, pp. 48–49; "Arizona Should Defend Itself," *Tucson Arizona Star*, April 27, 1957, clipping in Folder 3, Box IV, GEP, UNMGL.

2. Max Gubatayao, "Letters to the Editor," *America*, March 23, 1957, p. 689; *The New York Times*, March 25, 1957, p. 16.

3. *Congressional Record*, 85th Cong., 1st Sess., 103, Appendix, p. A1708; *The New York Times*, March 11, 1957, p. 19.

4. Sisseton meeting with Glenn Emmons, Minutes: Tribal Area Conferences, 1956, p. 11, Folder 2, Box III, GEP, UNMGL; Glenn Emmons to David T. Beals, December 31, 1956, Folder 1, Box V, GEP, UNMGL.

5. Glenn Emmons to William A. Ulman, July 15, 1957, Folder 12, Box IV, GEP, UNMGL; Papago meeting with Glenn Emmons, Minutes: Tribal Area Conferences, 1956, pp. 4–5, Folder 9, Box III, GEP, UNMGL; U.S., Congress, Senate, *Federal Indian Policy: Hearings Before the Subcommittee of the Committee on Interior and Insular Affairs, United States Senate, Eighty-fifth Congress, First Session, on S. 809, S. Con. Res. 3, and S. 331*, 1957, pp. 206–7.

6. Papago meeting with Emmons, p. 28; Glenn Emmons, "Industry Moves to Indian Country," *Industrial Development* (June, 1957), inserted by Republican Senator Barry Goldwater of Arizona into the *Congressional Record*, 85 Cong., 1 Sess., 103, Appendix, p. A5777; Alan L. Sorkin, "American Indians Industrialize to Combat Poverty," p. 23; U.S., Comptroller General of the United States, *Report to the Congress of the United States: Administration of Withdrawal Activities by the Bureau of Indian Affairs, Department of the Interior*, 1958, p. 41, Folder 4–B (2)—Bureau of Indian Affairs, 1956–60, Box 117, OF, CF, DDEL.

7. U.S., Department of the Interior, Glenn Emmons, "Bureau of Indian Affairs," *Secretary of the Interior Annual Reports*, 1956, pp. 208–9; Robert Young, *The Navajo Yearbook: 1951–1961, A Decade of Progress*, p. 192; Comptroller General, *Report to the Congress: Withdrawal Activities*, pp. 39, 41.

8. Comptroller General, *Report to the Congress: Withdrawal Activities*, p. 41; Young, *The Navajo Yearbook*, p. 192.

9. Comptroller General, *Report to the Congress: Withdrawal Activities*, p. 40, 43; Emmons, "Industry Moves to Indian Country," P. A5777; U.S., Department of the Interior, Glenn Emmons, "Bureau of Indian Affairs," *Secretary of the Interior Annual Reports*, 1957, pp. 246–47.

10. Emmons, "Bureau of Indian Affairs," 1957, pp. 246–47; Vince Pratt interview with George and Chuck Allen, Summer, 1971, tape 827; and Vince Pratt interview with Mae Eastman, July 28, 1971, tape 754, SDOHC, USD.

11. Emmons, "Bureau of Indian Affairs," 1957, p. 246; Comptroller General, *Report to the Congress: Withdrawal Activities*, pp. 40–43, 50.

12. Emmons, "Bureau of Indian Affairs," 1957, p. 246; Comptroller General, *Report to the Congress: Withdrawal Activities*, pp. 42–43.

13. Sorkin, "American Indians Industrialize," p. 21; Thomas H. Dodge, "Implementation of Commissioner's Memorandum of April 12, 1956, on Programming for Indian Social and Economic Improvement," p. 5, delivered before the Tri-Area Resources Conference in Phoenix, Arizona, January 27–29, 1958, transcript in Box 369 (68A–2045, 14/46: 48–5), RBIA, RG 75, NA.

14. Sorkin, "American Indians Industrialize," pp. 20–21; Comptroller General, *Report to the Congress: Withdrawal Activities*, pp. 40–41.

15. "The Bureau of Indian Affairs Voluntary Relocation Program," found in BIA to Sarah McClendon, March 16, p. 3, Folder 14, Box IV, GEP, UNMGL; Peter Dorner, "Needed: A New policy for the American Indians," p. 167; Robert A. White, "American Indian Crisis," pp. 207–8.

16. Senate, *Federal Indian Policy: Hearings on S. 809, S. Con. Res. 3, and S. 331*, pp. 3–4.

17. Ibid., pp. 1–4.

18. Ibid., pp. 1, 48–49.

19. Ibid., pp. 239–42.

20. Ibid., pp. 260–78.

21. *The New York Times*, April 12, 1957, p. 51, and April 22, 1957, p. 25.

22. *Congressional Record*, 85 Cong., 1 Sess., 103, pp. 5025–29; U.S., Congress, House, *Construction of Indian Hospitals: Hearings Before a Subcommittee of the Committee on Interstate and Foreign Commerce, United States House of Representatives, Eighty-fifth Congress, First Session, on H.R. 2021 and H.R. 2380*, 1957, p. 24.

23. House, *Construction of Indian Hospitals: Hearings*, pp. 5–6, 8.

24. *Congressional Record*, 85th Cong., 1st Sess., 103, p. 13958.

25. U.S., Congress, Senate, *Timber Sales—Quinaielt Reservation*, S. Rept. 971, 85th Cong., 1st Sess., 1957, pp. 2–4.

26. *Congressional Record*, 85th Cong., 2d Sess., 104, p. 8535; "Statement by the Department of the Interior concerning the 'Kaleidoscope' Television Program of November 16, 1958, on the American Indian," Folder—Indians (1), Box 12, FSP, ERF, DDEL.

27. *The New York Times*, December 8, 1957, p. 137, and March 31, 1958, p. 29.

## Chapter 8
## Termination in Action
## and Under Fire

1. Alan L. Sorkin, *American Indians and Federal Aid*, p. 158; William A. Brophy and Sophie D. Aberle, *The Indian: America's Unfinished Business*, pp. 195–96.

2. *The New York Times*, October 14, 1956, p. 71.

3. U.S., Congress, Senate, *Klamath Indian Tribe—Termination of Federal*

*Supervision: Hearings Before the Committee on Interior and Insular Affairs and Its Subcommittee on Indian Affairs, United States Senate, Eighty-fourth Congress, Second Session,* 1956, pp. 12, 21–22; Anthony Netboy, "Uproar on Klamath Reservation," p. 21.

4. Netboy, "Uproar on Klamath Reservation," p. 21; Senate, *Klamath Indian Tribe: Hearings,* p. 16.

5. Senate, *Klamath Indian Tribe: Hearings,* p. 12, 65–80.

6. Ibid., p. 14–15; U.S., Congress, House, *Amending the Klamath Termination Act: Hearings Before the Subcommittee on Indian Affairs of the Committee on Interior and Insular Affairs, House of Representatives, Eighty-fifth Congress, First Session, on H.R. 650, H.R. 663, H.R. 2471, and H.R. 2518,* 1957, p. 95.

7. House, *Amending the Klamath Termination Act: Hearings,* pp. 2–3; *Klamath meeting with Glenn Emmons, Minutes: Tribal Area Conferences, 1956,* pp. 1–3, Folder 12, Box III, GEP, UNMGL.

8. House, *Amending the Klamath Termination Act: Hearings,* pp. 5, 148–76.

9. U.S., Congress, House, Authorizing the United States to Defray the Cost of Assisting the Klamath Tribe of Indians to Prepare for Termination of Federal Supervision, and to Defer Sales of Tribal Property, H. Rept. 379 to Accompany S. 469, 85th Cong., 1st Sess., 1957, pp. 1–6, 26; Richard L. Neuberger, "Solving the Stubborn Klamath Dilemma," pp. 21–22.

10. "Sustained Yield vs. Continuous Growth," p. 4.

11. William B. Morse, "Land of the Wocus," p. 26, 54–56.

12. Mrs. Wade Crawford, "An Indian Talks Back," pp. 48–50.

13. Albert G. Hall, "Washington Lookout," p. 9.

14. U.S., Congress, Senate, *Amendments to the Klamath Termination Act of 1954: Hearings Before the Subcommittee on Indian Affairs of the Committee on Interior and Insular Affairs, United States Senate, Eighty-fifth Congress, First Session, on S. 2047,* Part 1, 1957, pp. 53–54, 70, 72–74, 150–51.

15. Ibid., pp. 9, 106–17, 129, 267–70.

16. Ibid., pp. 159–64.

17. U.S., Congress, Senate, *Amendments to the Klamath Termination Act of 1954: Hearings Before the Subcommittee on Indian Affairs of the Committee on Interior and Insular Affairs, United States Senate, Eighty-fifth Congress, Second Session, on S. 2047 and S. 3051,* Part 2, 1958, pp. 308–9, 339; "Seaton Outlines Klamath Indian Proposal to Congress," pp. 12–13.

18. "House Klamath Bill Needs Strengthening," *Oregon Journal,* July 31, 1958, inserted by Richard Neuberger into the *Congressional Record,* 85th Cong., 2d Sess., 104, p. 17568; "In the Day's News," *Klamath Herald and News,* March 23, 1958, inserted by Richard Neuberger into the *Congressional Record,* 85th Cong., 2d Sess., 104, pp. 5197–98.

19. "Sustained-Yield Issue," *Portland Oregonian,* August 1, 1958, inserted by Richard Neuberger into the *Congressional Record,* 85th Cong., 2d Sess., 104, pp. 17568; Don Magnuson, "How the Trick Was Turned," p. 8.

20. U.S., Congress, American Indian Policy Review Commission, *Report on Terminated and Nonfederally Recognized Indians,* 1976, pp. 57–59; *The New York Times,* July 2, 1961, p. 19, and August 30, 1964, p. 72; Brophy and Aberle, *The Indian,* p. 197.

21. Nancy Oestreich Lurie, "Menominee Termination: From Reservation to Colony," p. 262; U.S., Congress, House, *Authorizing Payment by the Federal Government of the Cost of Making Certain Studies Necessary to Assist the Menominee Tribe of Indians to Prepare for the Termination of Federal Supervision,* H. Rept. 2235 to Accompany H.R. 6218, 84th Cong., 2d Sess., 1956, p. 4.

22. David W. Ames and Burton R. Fisher, "The Menominee Termination Crisis: Barriers in the Way of a Rapid Cultural Transition," pp. 103–4, 1–8.

23. Ibid., p. 103; Patricia K. Ourada, *The Menominee Indians: A History,* pp. 196–97.

24. U.S., Congress, Senate, *Relating to the Plan for Control of the Property of the Menominee Indian Tribe and for Other Purposes,* S. Rept. 2412 to Accompany H.R. 9280, 84th Cong., 2d Sess., 1956, pp. 2–3, 6; Gary Orfield, "The Menominees and the Congress," *A Study of the Termination Policy,* p. 7.

25. Orfield, "The Shuffling of the Papers," Ibid., p. 12; idem., "The Wisconsin Idea," Ibid., pp. 6–7; idem., "The Menominees and the Congress," p. 8.

26. *Congressional Record,* 85th Cong., 2d Sess., 104, pp. 12078–79; Orfield, "The Menominees and the Congress," p. 8.

27. Ourada, *The Menominee Indians,* p. 196; Orfield, "The Response of the Tribe," *A Study of the Termination Policy,* pp. 14–15.

28. Orfield, "The Response of the Tribe," p. 18; idem., "The Wisconsin Idea," p. 7.

29. Orfield, "The Menominees and the Congress," pp. 8–9.

30. Lurie, "Menominee Termination," p. 263; Orfield, "The Response of the Tribe," pp. 18–19; Ourada, *The Menominee Indians,* p. 201.

31. Orfield, "The Response of the Tribe," p. 19; U.S., Department of the Interior, "Bureau of Indian Affairs," *Secretary of the Interior Annual Reports,* 1959, p. 245.

32. Orfield, "The Wisconsin Idea," pp. 11–12; Emmons, "Bureau of Indian Affairs," 1959, p. 245.

33. Emmons, "Bureau of Indian Affairs," 1959, p. 245; Orfield, "The Shuffling of the Papers," p. 15.

34. Orfield, "The Menominees and the Congress," p. 11.

35. Ibid., pp. 9–12.

36. Ourada, *The Menominee Indians,* pp. 203–4.

## Chapter 9
## Policy in Retreat

1. *Congressional Record,* 85th Cong., 1st Sess., 103, p. 15564; U.S., Congress, House, *California Indians, 1957: Hearings Before the Subcommittee of the Committee on Interior and Insular Affairs, House of Representatives, Eighty-fifth Congress, First Session, on H.R. 2576, H.R. 2824, H.R. 2838, and H.R. 6364,* 1957, pp. 1, 10, 12–19, 21–27, 30–38.

2. Roger Ernst to Fred Seaton (with attachments), February 14, 1958, Folder— BIA (articles), Box 9, FSP, ERF, DDEL; American Indian Development Foundation, "Statement of Objectives," pp. 2, 8, 12, 31, 34–A, Folder 3, Box V, GEP, UNMGL; Cherokee meeting with Glenn Emmons, Minutes: Tribal Area Conferences, 1956, pp. 25–27, Folder 4, Box III, GEP, UNMGL.

3. Colonel William Ulman to William Keeler, November 12, 1957, and Glenn Emmons to David T. Beals, December 3, 1957, Folder 1, Box V, GEP, UNMGL; Glenn Emmons to Russell C. Harrington, April 29, 1958, Folder 13, Box IV, GEP, UNMGL.

4. Colonel William Ulman to David T. Beals, January 17, 1958, and numerous letters from oil and oil-drilling equipment companies with contributions for the AIDF, Folder 1, Box V, GEP, UNMGL.

5. Glenn Emmons to Lester J. Norris, April 14, 1958, Folder 13, Box IV, GEP, UNMGL; K. Blyth Emmons to H. B. Jordan, March 28, 1958, K. Blyth Emmons to David T. Beals, July 18, 1958, Folder 2, Box V, GEP, UNMGL; Glenn Emmons to Larry Burt, March 10, 1976, correspondence in author's files.

6. Glenn Emmons to Newton Edwards, April 22, 1958, Folder 13, Box IV, GEP, UNMGL.

7. Ibid.; U.S., President, Proclamation, *Federal Register*, XXV, No. 121, March 12, 1958, p. 1699; U.S., Comptroller General of the United States, *Report to the Congress of the United States: Administration of Withdrawal Activities by the Bureau of Indian Affairs, Department of the Interior*, 1958, pp. 15–16, Folder 4–B (2)—Bureau of Indian Affairs, 1956–60, Box 117, OF, CF, DDEL.

8. Department of the Interior Information Service, "Land Sales Suspended on Crow Indian Reservation," Press Release for May 5, 1958, Folder—Indians (1), Box 12, FSP, ERF, DDEL; U.S., Department of the Interior, Glenn Emmons, "Bureau of Indian Affairs," *Secretary of the Interior Annual Reports*, 1959, p. 253.

9. U.S., Department of the Interior, Glenn Emmons, "Bureau of Indian Affairs," *Secretary of the Interior Annual Reports*, 1958, pp. 221–22.

10. Ibid., p. 221; *Executive Club News*, October 11, 1957, p. 5, clipping in Folder 8, Box II, GEP, UNMGL; BIA Press Release for July 17, 1958, inserted by Florida Congressman James A. Haley into the *Congressional Record*, 85th Cong., 2d Sess., CIV, Appendix, p. A6476.

11. U.S., Congress, Senate, *Area Redevelopment Act: Hearings Before a Subcommittee of the Committee on Banking and Currency, United States Senate, Eighty-sixth Congress, First Session, on S. 268, S. 722, and S. 1064*, 1959, pp. 122–23; *The New York Times*, September 21, 1958, p. 126.

12. U.S., Congress, House, *Department of the Interior and Related Agencies Appropriations for 1960: Hearings Before a Subcommittee of the Committee on Appropriations, United States House of Representatives, Eighty-sixth Congress, First Session*, 1959, p. 747. A good example of the type of article Emmons wrote for business magazines is his "Economic Progress of the American Indian."

13. U.S., Congress, Senate, *Area Redevelopment Act*, S. Rept. 1494 to Accompany S. 3683, 85th Cong., 2d Sess., 1958, pp. 1–2, 20, 31; U.S., Congress, House, *Area Redevelopment Act*, H. Rept. 360 to Accompany S. 722, 86th Cong., 1st Sess., 1959, p. 2.

14. Barton Greenwood to K. Blyth Emmons, July 7, 1958, Folder 13, Box IV, GEP, UNMGL; Glenn Emmons to K. Blyth Emmons, July 3, 1958, and Colonel William Ulman to David T. Beals, April 21, 1958, Folder 2, Box V, GEP, UNMGL.

15. Roger Ernst to Glenn Emmons, June 20, 1958, and Roger Ernst to Glenn Emmons, July 3, 1958, Folder 2, Box V, GEP, UNMGL.

16. U.S., Comptroller General of the United States, *Audit Report to the Congress of the United States: Administration of Indian Lands by the Bureau of Indian Affairs, Department of the Interior*, 1956, p. 29, 34, Folder 4–B (1)—Bureau of Indian Affairs, 1956–60, Box 117, OF, CF, DDEL.

17. Taos Pueblo meeting with Glenn Emmons, Minutes: Tribal Area Conferences, 1956, pp. 4–6, Folder 5, Box III, GEP, UNMGL, U.S., Congress, Senate, *Providing for the Restoration to Tribal Ownership of All Vacant and Undisposed-of-Ceded Lands on Certain Indian Reservations*, S. Rept. 1508 to Accompany H.R. 8544, 85th Cong., 2d Sess., 1958, pp. 1–3; Department of the Interior Information Service, "News Release," Press Release for July 8, 1959, Folder—Indian Affairs, Box 9, FSP, ERF, DDEL.

18. Department of the Interior Information Service, "News Release on Indian Policy," Press Release for September 13, 1958, Folder—BIA (articles), Box 9, FSP, ERF, DDEL.

19. Glenn Emmons to Don C. Foster, October 9, 1958, Folder 13, Box IV, GEP, UNMGL; Emmons "Bureau of Indian Affairs," 1959, p. 231.

20. *Hanford* (California) *Sentinel*, June 9, 1958, clipping in Folder 20, Box V, GEP, UNMGL.

21. Donald Kirkley, "Look and Listen," *Baltimore Sun*, November 18, 1958, clipping in Folder—Indian Affairs, Box 9, FSP, ERF, DDEL; Statement by the Department of the Interior concerning the "Kaleidoscope" Television Program of November 16, 1958, on the American Indian, Folder—Indians (1), Box 12, FSP, ERF, DDEL.

22. *Indian Affairs* (February 1959), n.p., reprinted in the *Congressional Record*, 86th Cong., 1st Sess., 105, p. 4856.

23. Ibid.; U.S., Congress, House, *Alaska Native Loan Program: Twenty-fifth Report by the Committee on Government Operations*, H. Rept. 1821, 85th Cong., 2d Sess., 1958, passim.

24. Glenn Emmons to Larry Burt, January 18, 1974, correspondence in author's files.

25. *United States Statutes at Large*, LI, 85–186, p. 468; Emmons, "Bureau of Indian Affairs," 1959, p. 253; Glenn Emmons, address before the eleventh annual Washington conference of the Association of State Planning and Development Agencies, March 23, 1960, pp. 17–18, transcript in Folder 14, Box II, GEP, UNMGL.

26. Emmons, address before the Association of State Planning and Development Agencies, pp. 18–19; Glenn Emmons, address at the dedication of a new school and a new industrial plant on the Eastern Cherokee Reservation, Cherokee, North Carolina, December 2, 1959, pp. 5–7, transcript in Folder 14, Box II, GEP, UNMGL.

27. Colonel William Ulman to Lester Norris, June 22, 1959, and Everett E. Hagen to Ben Reifel, October 9, 1959, Folder 2, Box V, GEP, UNMGL; Glenn Emmons to Everett E. Hagen, May 25, 1960, Folder 15, Box IV, GEP, UNMGL; Emmons to Burt, March 10, 1976.

28. *Congressional Record*, 86th Cong., 1st Sess., 105, pp. 1916, 1918; House, *Area Redevelopment Act*, pp. 3–7.

29. U.S., Congress, House, *Operation Bootstrap for the American Indian:*

*Hearings Before the Subcommittee on Indian Affairs of the Committee on Interior and Insular Affairs, House of Representatives, Eighty-sixth Congress, Second Session, on H.R. 7701, H.R. 8033, and H.R. 8590,* 1960, pp. 11–15, 18.

30. Ibid., pp. 16, 43, 51–52, 72–73, 82–83.

31. *Indian Views,* n.d., clipping in Folder 8, Box 5, GEP, UNMGL; *The New York Times,* January 12, 1957, p. 21, January 19, 1957, p. 11, and January 22, 1957, p. 24.

32. Jack D. H. Hays, Motion C-4152-PCT, Arizona District Court, n.d., copy in Folder 7, Box 5, GEP, UNMGL; *Arizona Republic,* May 5, 1959, clipping in Folder 8, Box V, GEP, UNMGL.

33. *Indian Views; The New York Times,* March 19, 1959, p. 35, and March 21, 1959, p. 14.

34. Harold Fey, "Indians Back Area Bill for Aid."

35. *The New York Times,* April 2, 1959, p. 25; "The United States Department of Justice and the Case of Brigadier General Herbert C. Holdridge (Retired) and the Navajo Tribe," May 3, 1959, pp. 2–4, Folder 9, Box V, GEP, UNMGL; John Yazzie to the Editor, *Arizona Republic,* May 13, 1959, clipping in Folder 8, Box V, GEP, UNMGL.

36. *Arizona Daily Sun,* June 25, 1959, clipping in Folder 8, Box V, GEP, UNMGL; "Statement of Paul Jones Relative to the Incident of Tuesday, April 21, 1959," Folder 7, Box V, GEP, UNMGL.

37. *Albuquerque Tribune,* May 2, 1959, clipping in Folder 8, Box V, GEP, UNMGL; "The United States Department of Justice and General Herbert C. Holdridge," p. 2.

38. Hays, Motion C–4152–PCT, n.p.; *Phoenix Gazette,* November 13, 1959, *Flagstaff Sun,* November 20, 1959, and *Winslow Mail,* February 26, 1960, clippings in Folder 8, Box V, GEP, UNMGL.

39. *The New York Times,* March 22, 1959, p. 43; March 25, 1959, p. 17; and June 26, 1960, p. 11; "Indians Appeal to U.S. Civil Rights Group"; "Indians Protest TV Misrepresentation."

40. *Albuquerque Tribune,* May 1, 1959, Folder 8, Box V, GEP, UNMGL; *The New York Times,* July 9, 1960, p. 2, and December 16, 1960, p. 25.

41. Morton H. Silver to Dwight D. Eisenhower, June 4, 1954, Box 147, GF, CF, DDEL.

42. Morton H. Silver to Dwight D. Eisenhower, June 26, 1954, Box 147, GF, CF, DDEL.

43. *Miami Herald,* March 23, 1956, clipping in Folder 18, Box III, GEP, UNMGL; "General History of Negotiations by Commissioner Glenn L. Emmons with the Everglades Miccosukee Indians of Florida, 1954–60," pp. 9–10, Folder 6, Box V, GEP, UNMGL.

44. Remarks by Glenn Emmons at the General Session, Gallup Area Conference, Minutes: Tribal Area Conferences, 1956, pp. 23–24, Folder 5, Box III, GEP, UNMGL; "General History of Negotiations with Miccosukee Indians," pp. 13–14.

45. "General History of Negotiations with Miccosukee Indians," pp. 14–16.

46. Ibid., pp. 18–23.

47. Fred Seaton to Glenn Emmons, February 4, 1959, Folder—Indian Affairs,

Box 9, FSP, ERF, DDEL; Glenn Emmons to Fred Seaton, May 27, 1959, Folder 14, Box IV, GEP, UNMGL.

48. Roger Ernst to Fred Seaton, August 23, 1960, Folder—Indian Affairs, Box 9, FSP, ERF, DDEL; "General History of Negotiations with Miccosukee Indians," pp. 29–31.

49. Glenn Emmons to LeRoy Collins, January 29, 1960, Folder 15, Box IV, GEP, UNMGL; "General History of Negotiations with Miccosukee Indians," pp. 34–40; James W. Covington, "Trail Indians of Florida," pp. 52–53.

50. Covington, "Trail Indians," pp. 53–55; *The New York Times*, September 25, 1960, p. 28.

## Chapter 10
## Conclusion

1. Glenn Emmons to Larry Burt, January 18, 1974, correspondence in author's files.

2. *Santa Fe New Mexican*, September 15, 1963, clipping in Folder 20, Box V, GEP, UNMGL; Glenn Emmons, *Freedom for the First Americans*, notes for a proposed book manuscript found in Folder 15, Box V, GEP, UNMGL.

3. U.S., Congress, Senate, *Indian Education: A National Tragedy—A National Challenge*, S. Rept. 501, 91st Cong., 2d Sess., 1969, pp. 14–15; *The New York Times*, March 16, 1961, p. 24.

4. D'Arcy McNickle, "The Indian Tests the Mainstream," p. 278; U.S., Department of the Interior, Philleo Nash, "Bureau of Indian Affairs," *Secretary of the Interior Annual Reports*, 1961, p. 277.

5. S. Lyman Tyler, *A History of Indian Policy*, pp. 205–6; Alan L. Sorkin, "American Indians Industrialize to Combat Poverty," p. 20.

6. Tyler, *Indian Policy*, pp. 198, 201–2, 206–13; Senate, *Indian Education*, pp. 15–16; Richard Schifter, "Trends in Federal Indian Administration," pp. 12–13.

7. D'Arcy McNickle, *Native American Tribalism: Indian Survivals and Renewals*, pp. vi–viii.

8. Arrell Morgan Gibson, *The American Indian: Prehistory to the Present*, pp. 561–63.

9. Patricia K. Ourada, *The Menominee Indians, A History*, pp. 204–8.

10. Ibid., pp. 208–20.

11. "A Paleface Uprising"; Peter Monkres, "The Longest Walk: An Indian Pilgrimage," pp. 350–51; M. J. Sobran, Jr., "Paleface Lib!"

12. Gibson, *The American Indian*, p. 570.

# Bibliography

## Manuscripts

Dwight D. Eisenhower Library. Ewald Research Files, Fred Seaton Papers.
———. General File, Central Files.
———. General File, Official Files.
University of New Mexico General Library. Glenn Emmons Papers.
National Archives. Record Group 75, Records of the Bureau of Indian Affairs.
    Most of the documents in this category still belong to the BIA and are lo-
    cated in the National Records Center in Suitland, Maryland. At some fu-
    ture date they will be deposited in the National Archives building and
    catalogued in the Record Group shown.
———. Record Group 220, American Indian Policy Review Commission.

## Interviews

Glenn Emmons to Larry Burt, January 18, 1974. Correspondence in author's
    files.
Glenn Emmons to Larry Burt, March 10, 1976. Correspondence in author's files.
Larry Burt interview with Walter McDonald, July 20, 1980.
Madison Coombs to Larry Burt, March 24, 1980. Tape in author's files.
Orme Lewis to Larry Burt, March 19, 1980. Correspondence in author's files.

The following interviews are located in the South Dakota Oral History Center
    at the University of South Dakota:

Anonymous interview by Joseph Cash (restricted use), August 25, 1967, tape
    18.
Vince Pratt interview with George and Chuck Allen, Summer, 1971, tape 827.
Joseph Cash interview with Louis Leader Charge, Summer, 1968, tape 76.
Joseph Cash interview with Charles E. Dawes, June 5, 1976, tape 1019.
Gerald Wolff interview with Lenora DeWitt, August 25, 1971, tape 786.
Herbert Hoover interview with Alfred DuBray, July 28, 1970, tape 533.
Vince Pratt interview with Oliver D. Eastman, August 3, 1971, tape 768.
Gerald Wolff interview with Clyde Gildersleeve, August 23, 1972, tape 876.
Joseph Cash interview with Jake Herman, Summer, 1967, tape 38.

Joseph Cash interview with Walter Gene Jennison, June 3, 1976, tape 1022.
Herbert Hoover interview with Gordon Jones, June 2, 1971, tape 684.
Cynthia Kelsey interview with Naomi Warren LaDue, August 14, 1968, tape
     224.
Willard Fraser interview with Eloise Pease, September 10, 1970, tape 599.
Joseph Cash interview with Purcell Rainwater, Summer 1967, tape 34.
Joseph Cash interview with Julis and Jack Rustemeyer, Summer 1967, tape 39.
Joseph Cash interview with Floyd E. Taylor, August 9, 1968, tape 50.
Gerald Wolff interview with Madline Eagle Thunder, September 2, 1971, tape
     801.

## Theses and Dissertations

Boender, Debra R. "Glenn Emmons of Gallup." M.A. thesis, University of New
     Mexico, 1976.
Fixico, Donald L. "Termination and Relocation: Federal Indian Policy in the
     1950s." Ph.D. dissertation, University of Oklahoma, 1980.
Hasse, Larry J. "Termination and Assimilation: Federal Indian Policy, 1943 to
     1961." Ph.D. dissertation, Washington State University, 1974.

## Federal Documents

*Congressional Record.* 1953–60.
U.S. Commission on Civil Rights. *Justice: 1961 United States Commission on
     Civil Rights.* Book 5, 1961.
U.S. Congress. *Agricultural Extension Work Among Indians, Transfer to the
     Department of Agriculture: Joint Hearings Before Subcommittees of the
     Committees on Interior and Insular Affairs, Eighty-third Congress, Second
     Session, on S. 3385 and H.R. 8982.* 1954.
———. American Indian Policy Review Commission. *Report on Terminated
     and Nonfederally Recognized Indians.* 1976.
———. *Termination of Federal Supervision Over Certain Tribes of Indians:
     Joint Hearings Before Subcommittees of the Committees on Interior and
     Insular Affairs, Eighty-third Congress, Second Session, on S. 2670 and H.R.
     7674.* Part 1, 1954.
———. *Termination of Federal Supervision Over Certain Tribes of Indians:
     Joint Hearings Before Subcommittees of the Committees on Interior and
     Insular Affairs, Eighty-third Congress, Second Session, on S. 2744, H.R.
     6282, and H.R. 6547.* Part 2, 1954.
———. *Termination of Federal Supervision Over Certain Tribes of Indians:
     Joint Hearings Before Subcommittees of the Committees on Interior and
     Insular Affairs, Eighty-third Congress, Second Session, on S. 2745 and H.R.
     7320.* Part 4, 1954.
———. *Termination of Federal Supervision Over Certain Tribes of Indians: Joint
     Hearings Before Subcommittees of the Committees on Interior and Insu-
     lar Affairs, Eighty-third Congress, Second Session, on S. 2745 and H.R.
     7320.* Part 4-A, 1954.

———. *Termination of Federal Supervision Over Certain Tribes of Indians: Joint Hearings Before Subcommittees of the Committees on Interior and Insular Affairs, Eighty-third Congress, Second Session, on S. 2749 and H.R. 7322.* Part 5, 1954.

———. *Termination of Federal Supervision Over Certain Tribes of Indians: Joint Hearings Before Subcommittees of the Committees on Interior and Insular Affairs, Eighty-third Congress, Second Session, on S. 2813, H.R. 2828, and H.R. 7135.* Part 6, 1954.

———. *Termination of Federal Supervision Over Certain Tribes of Indians: Joint Hearings Before Subcommittees of the Committees on Interior and Insular Affairs, Eighty-third Congress, Second Session, on S. 2750 and H.R. 7319.* Part 7, 1954.

———. *Termination of Federal Supervision Over Certain Tribes of Indians: Joint Hearings Before Subcommittees of the Committees on Interior and Insular Affairs, Eighty-third Congress, Second Session, on S. 2747 and H.R. 7321.* Part 8, 1954.

———. *Termination of Federal Supervision Over Certain Tribes of Indians: Joint Hearings Before Subcommittees of the Committees on Interior and Insular Affairs, Eighty-third Congress, Second Session, on H.R. 7981.* Part 9, 1954.

———. *Termination of Federal Supervision Over Certain Tribes of Indians: Joint Hearings Before Subcommittees of the Committees on Interior and Insular Affairs, Eighty-third Congress, Second Session, on H.R. 7552.* Part 10, 1954.

———. *Termination of Federal Supervision Over Certain Tribes of Indians: Joint Hearings Before Subcommittees of the Committees on Interior and Insular Affairs, Eighty-third Congress, Second Session, on S. 2743 and H.R. 7318.* Part 11, 1954.

———. *Termination of Federal Supervision Over Certain Tribes of Indians: Joint Hearings Before Subcommittees of the Committees on Interior and Insular Affairs, Eighty-third Congress, Second Session, on S. 2748 and H.R. 7316.* Part 12, 1954.

U.S. Congress, House. *Alaska Native Loan Program: Twenty-fifth Report by the Committee on Government Operations.* H. Rept. 1821, 85th Cong., 2d Sess., 1958.

———. *Amending the Klamath Termination Act: Hearings Before the Subcommittee on Indian Affairs of the Committee on Interior and Insular Affairs, House of Representatives, Eighty-fifth Congress, First Session, on H.R. 650, H.R. 663, H.R. 2471, and H.R. 2518.* 1957.

———. *Amending Title 18, United States Code, Entitled "Crimes and Criminal Procedures," With Respect to State Jurisdiction Over Offenses Committed by or Against Indians in the Indian Country, and to Confer on the State of California Civil Jurisdiction Over Indians in the State.* H. Rept. 848 to Accompany H.R. 1063, 83d Cong., 1st Sess., 1953.

———. *Area Redevelopment Act.* H. Rept. 360 to Accompany S. 722, 86th Cong., 1st Sess., 1959.

———. *Authorizing the Leasing of Restricted Indian Lands for Public, Religious,*

*Educational, Recreational, Residential, Business, and Other Purposes Requiring the Grant of Long-Term Leases.* H. Rept. 1562 to Accompany S. 34, 84th Cong., 1st Sess., 1955.

———. *Authorizing Payment by the Federal Government of the Cost of Making Certain Studies Necessary to Assist the Menominee Tribe of Indians to Prepare for the Termination of Federal Supervision.* H. Rept. 2235 to Accompany H.R. 6218, 84th Cong., 2d Sess., 1956.

———. *Authorizing the United States to Defray the Cost of Assisting the Klamath Tribe of Indians to Prepare for Termination of Federal Supervision, and to Deter Sales of Tribal Property.* H. Rept. 379 to Accompany S. 469, 85th Cong., 1st Sess., 1957.

———. *California Indians, 1957: Hearings Before the Subcommittee of the Committee on Interior and Insular Affairs, House of Representatives, Eighty-fifth Congress, First Session, on H.R. 2576, H.R. 2824, H.R. 2838, and H.R. 6364.* 1957.

———. *Construction of Indian Hospitals: Hearings Before a Subcommittee of the Committee on Interstate and Foreign Commerce, United States House of Representatives, Eighty-fifth Congress, First Session, on H.R. 2021 and H.R. 2380.* 1957.

———. *Department of the Interior and Related Agencies Appropriations for 1957: Hearings Before the Subcommittee of the Committee on Appropriations, United States House of Representatives, Eighty-fourth Congress, Second Session.* 1956.

———. *Department of the Interior and Related Agencies Appropriations for 1958: Hearings Before a Subcommittee of the Committee on Appropriations, United States House of Representatives, Eighty-fifth Congress, First Session.* 1957.

———. *Department of the Interior and Related Agencies Appropriations for 1960: Hearings Before a Subcommittee of the Committee on Appropriations, United States House of Representatives, Eighty-sixth Congress, First Session.* 1959.

———. *Department of the Interior and Related Agencies Appropriations for 1961: Hearings Before a Subcommittee of the Committee on Appropriations, United States House of Representatives, Eighty-sixth Congress, Second Session.* 1960.

———. *Directing the Secretary of the Interior to Conduct a Study and Investigation of Indian Education in the United States.* H. Rept. 2381 to Accompany H.J. Res. 451, 84th Cong., 2d Sess., 1956.

———. *Information on Removal of Restrictions on American Indians: A Memorandum and Accompanying Information from the Chairman of the Committee on Interior and Insular Affairs, House of Representatives, to Members of the Committee.* Committee Print 38, 88th Cong., 2d Sess., 1964.

———. *Interior Department Appropriations for 1955: Hearings Before the Subcommittee of the Committee on Appropriations, House of Representatives, Eighty-third Congress, Second Session.* 1954.

———. *Interior Department and Related Agencies Appropriations for 1956: Hearings Before the Subcommittee of the Committee on Appropriations, House of Representatives, Eighty-fourth Congress, First Session.* 1955.

————. *Operation Bootstrap for the American Indian: Hearings Before the Subcommittee on Indian Affairs of the Committee on Interior and Insular Affairs, House of Representatives, Eighty-sixth Congress, Second Session, on H.R. 7701, H.R. 8033, and H.R. 8590.* 1960.

————. *Providing a Certificate or Decree of Competency for U.S. Indians in Certain Cases.* H. Rept. 836 to Accompany H.R. 4985, 83d Cong., 1st Sess., 1953.

————. *Providing for the Termination of Federal Supervision Over the Property of Certain Tribes, Bands, and Colonies of Indians in the State of Utah and the Individual Members Thereof.* H. Rept. 2661 to Accompany S. 2670, 83d Cong., 2d Sess., 1954.

————. *Providing for the Termination of Federal Supervision Over the Property of Certain Tribes and Bands of Indians Located in Western Oregon, and the Individual Members Thereof.* H. Rept. 2492 to Accompany S. 2746, 83d Cong., 2d Sess., 1954.

————. *Providing for the Termination of Federal Supervision Over the Property of the Klamath Tribe of Indians Located in the State of Oregon and the Individual Members Thereof.* H. Rept. 2483 to Accompany S. 2745, 83d Cong., 2d Sess., 1954.

————. *Providing for the Termination of Federal Supervision Over the Property of the Peoria Tribe of Indians in the State of Oklahoma and the Individual Members Thereof.* H. Rept. 2802 to Accompany S. 3968, 84th Cong., 2d Sess., 1956.

————. *Providing for the Termination of Federal Supervision Over the Property of the Wyandotte Tribe of Oklahoma and the Individual Members Thereof.* H. Rept. 2804 to Accompany S. 3970, 84th Cong., 2d Sess., 1956.

————. *Providing Vocational Training for Adult Indians.* H. Rept. 2532 to Accompany H.R. 9904, 84th Cong., 2d Sess., 1956.

————. *Second Supplemental Appropriation Bill, 1956.* H. Rept. 1897 to Accompany H.R. 10004, 84th Cong. 2d Sess., 1956.

————. *Supplemental Appropriation Bill, 1955.* H. Rept. 2663 to Accompany H.R. 9936, 83d Cong., 2d Sess., 1954.

————. *The Supplemental Appropriation Bill, 1955: Hearings Before Subcommittees of the Committee on Appropriations, House of Representatives, Eighty-third Congress, Second Session.* 1954.

————. *Transferring the Maintenance and Operation of Hospital and Health Facilities For Indians to the Public Health Service.* H. Rept. 870 to Accompany H.R. 303, 83d Cong., 1st Sess., 1953.

U.S. Congress. Senate. *Amending the Act Entitled "To Confer Jurisdiction on the States of California, Minnesota, Nebraska, Oregon and Wisconsin, With Respect to Criminal Offenses and Civil Causes of Action Committed or Arising on Indian Reservations Within Such States."* S. Rept. 357 to Accompany S. 51, 84th Cong., 1st Sess., 1955.

————. *Amendments to the Klamath Termination Act of 1954: Hearings Before the Subcommittee on Indian Affairs of the Committee on Interior and Insular Affairs, United States Senate, Eighty-fifth Congress, First Session, on S. 2047.* Part 1, 1957.

————. *Amendments to the Klamath Termination Act of 1954: Hearings Be-

*fore the Subcommittee on Indian Affairs of the Committee on Interior and Insular Affairs, United States Senate, Eighty-fifth Congress, Second Session, on S. 2047 and S. 3051. Part 2, 1958.*

———. *Area Redevelopment Act.* S. Rept. 1494 to Accompany S. 3683, 85th Cong., 2d Sess., 1958.

———. *Area Redevelopment Act: Hearings Before a Subcommittee of the Committee on Banking and Currency, United States Senate, Eighty-sixth Congress, First Session, on S. 268, S. 722, and S. 1064. 1959.*

———. *Attorney Contracts with Indian Tribes.* S. Rept. 8, 83d Cong., 1st Sess., 1953.

———. *Federal Indian Policy: Hearings Before the Subcommittee of the Committee on Interior and Insular Affairs, United States Senate, Eighty-fifth Congress, First Session, on S. 809, S. Con. Res. 3, and S. 331. 1957.*

———. *Hearings Before a Subcommittee of the Committee on Appropriations: Interior Department Appropriations for 1954, United States Senate, Eighty-third Congress, First Session, on H.R. 4828. 1953.*

———. *Indian Education: A National Tragedy—A National Challenge.* S. Rept. 501, 91st Cong., 2d Sess., 1969.

———. *Interior Department Appropriations for 1955: Hearings Before a Subcommittee on Appropriations, United States Senate, Eighty-third Congress, Second Session, on H.R. 8680. 1954.*

———. *Interior Department and Related Agencies Appropriations for 1956: Hearings Before a Subcommittee of the Committee on Appropriations, United States Senate, Eighty-fourth Congress, First Session, on H.R. 5085. 1955.*

———. *Interior Department and Related Agencies Appropriations for 1957: Hearings Before a Subcommittee of the Committee on Appropriations, United States Senate, Eighty-fourth Congress, Second Session, on H.R. 9390. 1956.*

———. *Juvenile Delinquency (Indians): Hearings Before the Subcommittee to Investigate Juvenile Delinquency of the Committee on the Judiciary, United States Senate, Eighty-third Congress, Second Session, Pursuant to S. Res. 89. 1954.*

———. *Juvenile Delinquency (Indians): Hearings Before the Subcommittee to Investigate Juvenile Delinquency of the Committee on the Judiciary, United States Senate, Eighty-fourth Congress, First Session, Pursuant to S. Res. 62. 1955.*

———. *Juvenile Delinquency Among the Indians: Report of the Committee on the Judiciary, United States Senate, Made by Its Subcommittee to Investigate Juvenile Delinquency Pursuant to S. Res. 62 as Extended.* S. Rept. 1483, 84th Cong., 2d Sess., 1956.

———. *Klamath Indian Tribe—Termination of Federal Supervision: Hearings Before the Committee on Interior and Insular Affairs and Its Subcommittee on Indian Affairs, United States Senate, Eighty-fourth Congress, Second Session. 1956.*

———. *Nomination of Glenn L. Emmons: Hearings Before the Committee on Interior and Insular Affairs, United States Senate, Eighty-third Congress, First Session. 1953.*

———. *Providing for the Restoration to Tribal Ownership of All Vacant and Undisposed-of Ceded Lands on Certain Indian Reservations.* S. Rept. 1508 to Accompany H.R. 8544, 85th Cong., 2d Sess., 1958.

———. *Relating to the Plan for Control of the Property of the Menominee Indian Tribe and for Other Purposes.* S. Rept. 2412 to Accompany H.R. 9280, 84th Cong., 2d Sess., 1956.

———. *Relative to Employment for Certain Adult Indians on or near Indian Reservations.* S. Rept. 2664 to Accompany S. 3416, 84th Cong., 2d Sess., 1956.

———. *Second Supplemental Appropriation Bill, 1956: Hearings Before the Committee on Appropriations, United States Senate, Eighty-fourth Congress, Second Session, on H.R. 10004.* 1956.

———. *Termination of Federal Supervision Over the Property of the Klamath Tribe, Oregon.* S. Rept. 1631, 83rd Cong., 2d Sess., 1954.

———. *Timber Sales—Quinaielt Indian Reservation.* S. Rept. 971, 85th Cong., 1st Sess., 1957.

———. *Transferring the Maintenance and Operation of Hospital and Health Facilities for Indians to the Public Health Service.* S. Rept. 1530, 83d Cong., 2d Sess., 1954.

U.S. Department of the Interior. *Secretary of the Interior Annual Reports.* 1953–61.

## Articles

Abbott, George W. "The American Indian, Federal Citizen and State Citizen." *Federal Bar Journal,* 20 (1960): 248–60.

Ablon, Joan. "American Indian Relocation: Problems of Dependency and Management in the City." *Phylon* 26 (1965): 362–71.

Ames, David W., and Fisher, Burton R. "The Menominee Termination Crisis: Barriers in the Way of a Rapid Cultural Transition." *Human Organization* 18 (1959): 101–11.

Arnold, Oren. "The Navajo Wind That Speaks." *American Mercury,* December 1956, pp. 132–36.

Benge, William B. "Law and Order on Indian Reservations." *Federal Bar Journal* 20 (1960): 223–29.

Berger, Edward B. "Indian Lands—Minerals—Related Problems." *Rocky Mountain Mineral Law Institute* 14 (1968): 89–122.

———. "Negotiations for Acquiring Exploration Rights on Indians Lands." *Rocky Mountain Mineral Law Institute* 19 (1974): 447–81.

Bigart, Robert James. "Indian Culture and Industrialization." *American Anthropologist* 74 (1972): 1180–88.

Bohn, Dorothy. " 'Liberating' the Indian: Euphemism for a Land Grab." *Nation,* February 20, 1954, pp. 150–51.

"Broken Arrow." *Time,* March 4, 1957, pp. 48–49.

Chambers, Reid Peyton, and Price, Monroe E. "Discretion and the Leasing of Indian Lands." *Stanford Law Review* 26(1974):1061–95.

Collier, John. "Back to Dishonor?" *Christian Century,* May 12, 1954, pp. 578–80.

———. "Indian Takeaway: Betrayal of a Trust." *Nation*, October 2, 1954, pp. 290–91.

———. "The Unfinished Indian Wars." *Nation*, May 25, 1957, pp. 458–59.

"Consultation or Consent?" *Christian Century*, January 25, 1956, pp. 103–4.

Cooper, Charles. "New Hope." *American Forests*, September 1955, pp. 24–26, 51.

Covington, James W. "Trail Indians of Florida." *Florida Historical Quarterly* 58 (1979):37–57.

Crawford, Mrs. Wade. "An Indian Talks Back." *American Forests*, July 1957, pp. 4, 48–50.

Davies, Glen E. "State Taxation on Indian Reservations." *Utah Law Review*, 1966 (July 1966):132–51.

Dean, William. "Klamath Hearings in Oregon." *American Forests*, November 1957, pp. 12, 65–67.

Deer, Ada. "Menominee Restoration: How the Good Guys Won." *Journal of Intergroup Relations* 3 (September 1974): 41–50.

Dorner, Peter. "Needed: A New Policy for the American Indians." *Land Economics* 37 (1961): 162–73.

Emmons, Glenn. "Economic Progress of the American Indian." *Michigan Business Review*, November 1958, pp. 1–5.

———. "Future Prospects in Indian Affairs." *Indian Truth*, (January–February 1954, pp. 1–5.

———. "U.S. Aim: Give Indians a Chance." *Nation's Business*, July 1955, pp. 40–43, 51–53.

Fey, Harold E. "Indian Winter." *Christian Century*, March 2, 1955, pp. 265–67.

———. "Indians Back Area Bill for Aid." *Christian Century*, April 1, 1959, p. 382.

———. "Navajo Race With Tragedy." *Christian Century*, May 25, 1955, pp. 617–19.

———. "Record Interest in American Indians." *Christian Century*, May 23, 1956, p. 637.

———. "What Indians Want." *Christian Century*, September 21, 1955, pp. 1079–81.

Gilbert, William H., and Taylor, John L. "Indian Land Questions." *Arizona Law Review* 8 (1966):102–31.

Gilliland, Minnio. " 'Your Children Shall Learn Paper': A Report on Navajo Education." *National Education Association Journal* 45 (1956):558–60.

Goldberg, Carole E. "Public Law 280: The Limits of State Jurisdiction Over Reservation Indians." *UCLA Law Review* 22(1975):535–94.

Haas, Theodore H. "The Legal Aspects of Indian Affairs from 1887 to 1957." *Annals of the American Academy of Political and Social Science* 311(May 1957):12–22.

Hall, Albert G. "Washington Lookout." *American Forests*, June 1957, p. 9.

Harmer, Ruth Mulvey. "Uprooting the Indian." *Atlantic Monthly*, March 1956, pp. 54–57.

Hood, Susan. "Termination of the Klamath Indian Tribe of Oregon." *Ethnohistory* 19(1972):379–92.

"Indians Appeal to U.S. Civil Rights Group." *Christian Century*, April 8, 1959, p. 413.

"Indians Protest TV Misrepresentation." *Christian Century*, February 10, 1960, p. 157.

"Indians Resist Land Grabs." *Christian Century*, December 10, 1958, pp. 1421–22.

"Indians Still Losing Their Land." *Christian Century*, October 1, 1958, pp. 1102–3.

Jenkins, Bill. "Klamath Water Big Cog in Oregon's Prospects." *American Forests*, March 1958, pp. 24, 46.

Kelly, Lawrence. "The Indian Reorganization Act: The Dream and the Reality." *Pacific Historical Review* 44 (1975):291–312.

Kinney, J. P. "Will the Indian Make the Grade?" *American Forests*, December 1954, pp. 24–27, 52.

La Farge, Oliver. "The Enduring Indian." *Scientific American* 202 (February 1960):37–44.

———. "Termination of Federal Supervision: Disintegration and the American Indians." *Annals of the American Academy of Political and Social Science* 311(May 1957):41–46.

Lindley, Lawrence E. "Why Indians Need Land." *Christian Century*, November 6, 1957, pp. 1316–18.

Lurie, Nancy Oestreich. "The Indian Claims Commission Act." *Annals of the American Academy of Political and Social Science* 311 (May 1957): 56–70.

———. "Menominee Termination: From Reservation to Colony." *Human Organization* 31(1972):257–69.

McNickle, D'Arcy. "The Indian Tests the Mainstream." *Nation*, September 26, 1966, pp. 275–79.

———. "It's Almost Never Too Late." *Christian Century*, February 20, 1957, pp. 227–29.

———. "U.S. Indian Speaks." *Americas*, March, 1954, pp. 9–11, 27.

Magnuson, Don. "How the Trick Was Turned." *American Forests*, September 1958, p. 8.

Metcalf, Lee. "The Need for Revision of Federal Policy in Indian Affairs." *Indian Truth*, January–March 1958, pp. 1–8.

Mirrielees, Edith R. "The Cloud of Mistrust." *Atlantic Monthly*, February 1957, pp. 55–59.

Monkres, Peter. "The Longest Walk: An Indian Pilgrimage." *Christian Century*, April 5, 1978, pp. 350–52.

Morse, William B. "Land of the Wocus." *American Forests*, June 1957, pp. 24–26, 54–56.

Netboy, Anthony. "Uproar on Klamath Reservation." *American Forests*, January 1957, pp. 20–21, 61–62.

Neuberger, Richard. "How Oregon Rescued a Forest." *Harper's Magazine*, April 1959, pp. 48–52.

———. "Solving the Stubborn Klamath Dilemma." *American Forests*, pp. 20–22, 40–42.

Pomeroy, Kenneth B. "Unplanned Policies." *American Forests*, May 1957, pp. 24–27, 62–64.

"A Paleface Uprising." *Newsweek*, April 10, 1978, pp. 39–40.

"Propose to Enlarge Indian Loan Fund." *Christian Century*, June 24, 1959, pp. 740–41.

Rosenthal, Elizabeth. "Catching History by the Coattails." *Christian Century*, May 25, 1960, pp. 634–35.

Sawyer, Robert W. "Klamath Timber Should Be in National Forests." *American Forests*, March 1958, pp. 25–26, 47.

Schifter, Richard. "Trends in Federal Indian Administration." *South Dakota Law Review* 15(1970):1–21.

"Seaton Outlines Klamath Indian Proposal to Congress." *American Forests*, February 1958, pp. 12–13, 38–39.

Sobran, M. J., Jr. "Paleface Lib!" *National Review* 26(1974):1161.

Sonosky, Marvin J. "Oil, Gas, and Other Minerals on Indian Reservations." *Federal Bar Journal* 20(1960):230–34.

Sorkin, Alan L. "American Indians Industrialize to Combat Poverty." *Monthly Labor Review*, March 1969, pp. 19–25.

———. "The Economic and Social Status of the American Indian, 1940–1970." *Nebraska Journal of Economics* 22(Spring 1974):33–50.

Stocker, Joseph. "Trailer Teachers in Navajoland." *Arizona Highways*, August 1957, pp. 26–29.

"Sustained Yield vs. Continuous Growth." *American Forests*, August 1958, p. 4.

Talney, Mark A. "Question Validity of Klamath Plan." *Christian Century*, July 25, 1956, pp. 882–84.

Van de Mark, Dorothy, "The Raid on the Reservation." *Harper's Magazine*, March 1956, pp. 48–53.

Watkins, Arthur. "Termination of Federal Supervision: The Removal of Restrictions Over Indian Property and Person." *Annals of the American Academy of Political and Social Science* 311(May 1957):47–55.

White, Robert A. "American Indian Crisis." *Social Order* 11(May 1961):201–11.

Zimmerman, William, Jr. "The Role of the Bureau of Indian Affairs Since 1933." *Annals of the American Academy of Political and Social Science* 311(May 1957):31–40.

## Books

Berkhofer, Robert F., Jr. *The White Man's Indian: Images of the American Indian from Columbus to the Present.* New York: Alfred A. Knopf, 1978.

Brophy, William A., and Aberle, Sophie D. *The Indian: America's Unfinished Business.* Norman: University of Oklahoma Press, 1966.

Debo, Angie. *A History of the Indians of the United States.* Norman:University of Oklahoma Press, 1970.

Gibson, Arrell Morgan. *The American Indian: Prehistory to the Present.* Lexington, Mass.: D. C. Heath and Co., 1980.

Goldman, Eric F. *The Crucial Decade and After, 1945–1960.* New York: Vintage Books, 1960.

Kvasnicka, Robert M., and Viola, Herman J., eds. *The Commissioners of Indian Affairs, 1824–1977.* Lincoln: University of Nebraska Press, 1979.

Levine, Stuart, and Lurie, Nancy Oestreich, eds. *The American Indian Today.* Baltimore: Penguin Books, 1965.

Madigan, LaVerne. *The American Indian Relocation Program.* New York: American Association of Indian Affairs, 1956.

McNickle, D'Arcy. *Native American Tribalism: Indian Survivals and Renewals.* New York: Oxford University Press, 1973.

Meriam, Lewis, ed. *The Problems of Indian Administration.* Baltimore: Johns Hopkins Press, Institute for Government Research, 1928.

Nash, Gerald D. *The American West in the Twentieth Century: A Short History of an Urban Oasis.* 1973. Reprint. Albuquerque: University of New Mexico Press, 1977.

Orfield, Gary. *A Study of the Termination Policy.* Denver: National Congress of American Indians, 1965.

Ourada, Patricia K. *The Menominee Indians: A History.* Norman: University of Oklahoma Press, 1979.

Parman, Donald. *The Navajos and the New Deal.* New Haven: Yale University Press, 1976.

Philp, Kenneth. *John Collier's Crusade for Indian Reform: 1920–1954.* Tucson: University of Arizona Press, 1977.

Shafer, Boyd C. *Nationalism:Its Nature and Interpreters.* Washington, D.C.: American Historical Association, 1976.

Sorkin, Alan L. *American Indians and Federal Aid.* Washington, D.C.: Brookings Institution, 1971.

Steiner, Stan. *The New Indians.* New York: Delta, 1968.

Szasz, Margaret Connell. *Education and the American Indian: The Road to Self-Determination Since 1928.* Albuquerque: University of New Mexico Press, 1977.

Taylor, Graham D. *The New Deal and American Indian Tribalism: The Administration of the Indian Reorganization Act, 1934–45.* Lincoln: University of Nebraska Press, 1980.

Taylor, Theodore W. *The States and Their Indian Citizens.* Washington, D.C.: Department of the Interior, 1972.

Tyler, Lyman S. *A History of Indian Policy.* Washington, D.C.: United States Department of the Interior, 1973.

———. *Indian Affairs: A Work Paper on Termination With an Attempt to Show Its Antecedents.* Provo, Ut.: Institute of American Indian Studies, 1964.

Waddell, Jack O., and Watson, O. Michael, eds. *The American Indian in Urban Society.* Boston: Little, Brown, and Co., 1971.

Washburn, Wilcomb E. *The Assault on Indian Tribalism: The General Allotment Law (Dawes Act) of 1887.* Philadelphia: J. B. Lippincott, 1975.

———., ed. *The American Indian and the United States: A Documentary History.* vol. 3. New York: Random House, 1973.

Young, Robert W. *The Navajo Yearbook: 1951–1961, A Decade of Progress.* Window Rock, Ariz.: Bureau of Indian Affairs, 1961.

# Index